ZenDoodle Drawing Book

How to create amazing doodle forms

by Isobel Mann

Table of Contents

Introduction

Chapter 1 – How to draw doodle flowers

Chapter 2 – How to draw doodle dog

Chapter 3 – How to draw a cat

Chapter 4 – How to draw a doodle fish

Chapter 5 – How to draw doodle flower

Chapter 6 – How to draw a doodle skull

Chapter 7 – How to draw a doodle fish

Conclusion

Disclaimer

While all attempts have been made to verify the information provided in this book, the author does assume any responsibility for errors, omissions, or contrary interpretations of the subject matter contained within. **The information provided in this book is for educational and entertainment purposes only. The reader is responsible for his or her own actions and the author does not accept any responsibilities for any liabilities or damages, real or perceived, resulting from the use of this information.**

The trademarks that are used are without any consent, and the publication of the trademark is without permission or backing by the trademark owner. All trademarks and brands within this book are for clarifying purposes only and are the owned by the owners themselves, not affiliated with this document.

Introduction

Do you want to doodle and draw in your extra time? Ever felt that you could profit from your doodle drawings? That is precisely what various people are doing the world over right now, people simply like you.

I am a doodler! I generally have been and most likely dependably will be. In my doodling profession I have learned some valuable tips. I thought maybe it might be useful to bind them here. They positively helped me.

Doodle Tip 1:

Have some good times! This is not a genuine thing and nobody will be hurt on the off chance that you are not great. Simply release yourself and be pleased by what your hand produces!

Doodle Tip 2:

Mean to add a thought to your doodle with the examples you pick. For example I once drew a skull (exceptionally alarming) yet filled it with little hearts and blossom designs (extremely twee). The juxtaposition entertained me. I went searching for it and discovered it. So here it is:

Doodle Tip 3:

Doodle on great paper. From time to time, you will make a magnum opus. It will be a genuine compassion in the event that it is in the edge of the phone directory!

"Be that as it may, I doodle when I am on the telephone," you say. So keep a perfect cushion of good paper close you generally!

I mean dependably! I have a few: around my work area, in my handbag, by my overnight boardinghouse the auto!

Doodle Tip 4:

In the event that an immaculate white page is staying there startling you, simply shut your eyes and draw a squiggle on it. Presently it is "demolished". It can just show signs of improvement from here on in. This is an extraordinary approach to fake out your own particular personality. It is just the gab inside your head that says the page needs to end up being a perfect work of art - overlook your psyche and appreciate the procedure!

Doodle Tip 5:

Have a go at doodling with truly thin markers. Attempt some that is 1.0, 0.5, 0.3 and even 0.1 It is extremely fascinating how the distinctive thicknesses deliver altogether different sentiments when you draw. You get the chance to play and make sense of which one suits you best today.

Doodle Tip 6:

Play the scrawl amusement. Get somebody to simply do a basic scrawl on a bit of paper for you. At that point you take it back and turn it about until the picture appears to you. You can include a level of fun, by motivating them to name an animal, say a pooch or elephant or fish, and after that you need to figure out how to transform the scrawl into that!

Let's face honest, can be genuinely addictive when you're somewhat exhausted. Either while you're sat on the transport with a magazine, at takes a shot at your meal break or sat in a classroom with a notebook. These are all impeccable times to begin a magnificent doodle. My undisputed top choice is on the telephone, in some cases I just can't resist the urge to draw on the telephone directory or a post it note while I'm talking without end. There are numerous doodle implications, yet my clarification is it assists me with considering! At whatever point I complete a doodle I jump at the chance to spare it someplace, despite the fact that it's just taken me perhaps a couple of minutes to finish they hold some sort of quality that keeps me from discarding it! I some of the time take the thoughts I have caught in my doodle and start a greater drawing on a sketchbook. This is on the grounds that I feel the doodle can possibly turn into a pleasant bit of fine art.

Likewise in case need somewhat additional money every month offering your drawings online is an incredible strategy to help your month to month pay. I'm so happy I've go over this strategy as it has permitted me to take one of my distractions and transform it into something gainful. This is the reason I need to impart it to you. On the off chance that you can bear to set aside some extra time every day, you'll have the capacity to begin. In a matter of moments you'll have the capacity to effectively offer your snappy sketches and drawings on the web. The main drawing I sold was of a butterfly; from that point forward I have been drawing numerous types. What's extraordinary is that my inspiration to sketch expanded as I turned out to be more certain about my capacity. As I saw that people were really purchasing my drawings this gave me the certainty to go ahead. You will discover to that will your certainty increment as well as with each drawing you make you are likewise turning out to be more experience and adding to your drawing capacity.

So in case you're similar to me and like to doodle and draw, why not begin and figure out how to offer your drawings and doodles online today. Regardless of on the off chance that you are just barely beginning you're drawing profession, there are people scanning web searching for thoughts, thoughts that you may have accidentally made while you're doodling!

Doodle what you listen. A fun approach to free partner while you're doodling is to listen to whatever your educator or the people around you are stating and to doodle the things that you're finding out about. Here are a few approaches to doodle what you listen:

Doodle a verifiable figure. In the event that your instructor is discussing George Washington, draw him in an assortment of stances.

Doodle a man you've never met. In the event that you hear two people talking about a man with a clever name, simply envision what he would look like and draw him.

Doodle an idea. What do you think of when your educator says, "ban" or "ringer bend"? You don't need to doodle what the article really is - simply doodle what it makes you picture in your mind.

Doodle a melody. Did somebody stroll into the classroom with that melody that dependably gets latched onto your subconscious mind blasting from his earphones? Draw whatever it is the melody makes you think about.

Doodle a cityscape. Cityscapes are enjoyable to doodle and are ideal for the base or top edges of your pages. Draw a cityscape along the highest point of your scratch pad page, and have a ton of fun including the greater part of the little subtle elements that make it novel. Here are a few things you can do when you doodle a cityscape:

Make it night. The city looks the most wonderful around evening time, so draw a full moon and shade the sky in a dull shading.

Draw little windows in the houses' majority. Some will be lit and some won't be.

Include more subtle elements. Include trees, lights, telephone corners, waste jars, and even people walking their puppies on the streets outside the city.

Draw a city you adore. Think you know precisely what the New York cityscape resembles? Take a stab at drawing it and perceive how exact you were later.

Make your own particular doodle world. As you turn into a more experienced doodler, you can make your own particular world, with your own people, your own particular creatures, your own particular structures, and your own trees in it. As you turn out to be more encountered, your animals, musings, and people will start to tackle their own particular structure and everybody will have the capacity to remember them as yours.

Once you're an expert doodler, you can spread your affection for doodling to others. Turned into an after-school doodle mentor and impart your adoration for doodling to others.

You can even name your own particular world something like, "Megland," or "Walt's World," and compose this name on top of your doodles.

You can make a montage of your doodles in your room by taping the pages to your divider and being pleased with all the doodling you've done.

Doodle your name. Your name is another well known thing to doodle. There are an assortment of approaches to doodle your name, whether you're composing it again and again in the same way, or composing your name in a totally new manner without fail. Here are a few approaches to doodle your name:

Compose your name in cursive. Have a go at composing it with misrepresented circles.

Have a go at composing your name as little as you can while making it still clear.

Compose your first name alongside the last name of your smash. This will assist you with checking whether you're a match made in paradise.

Compose your name in huge square letters. Design the piece letters with vines, stars, planets, or hearts.

Compose your name in air pocket letters. Have cleanser air pockets drifting off the highest point of your name.

Doodle faces. Appearances are more confounded to draw than most flowers, however you'll feel compensated when you've genuinely learned to draw a face. You can draw the substance of your educator or your cohort, or simply have a great time drawing an arbitrary face. Here are some different approaches to doodle faces:

Work on drawing very nearly the same face with diverse looks. This will assist you with becoming acquainted with the face you're doodling.

Chapter 1 – How to draw doodle flowers

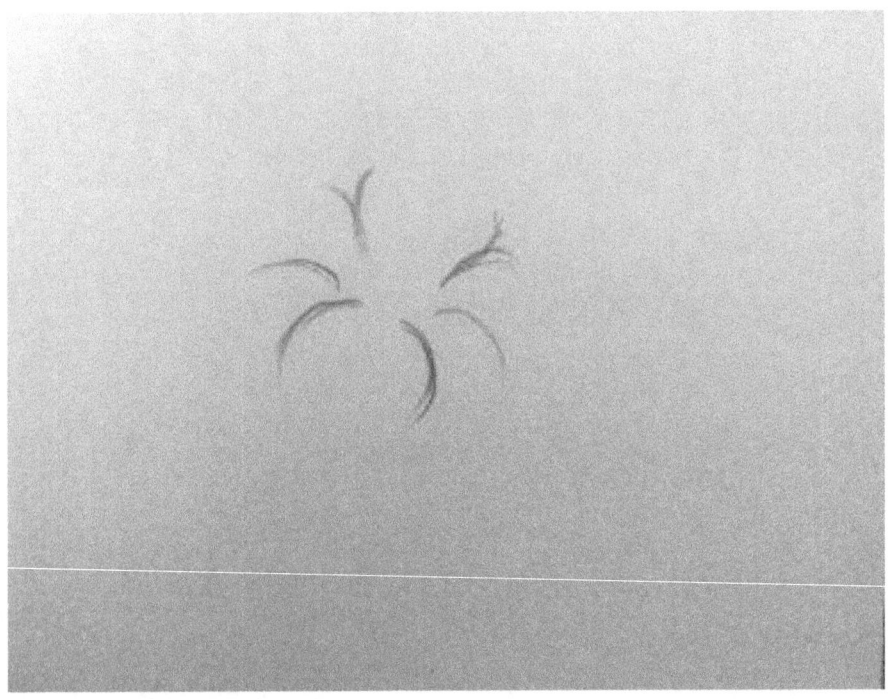

Step 1: How about we begin with three balls for the rose buds, then sketch in the rules for the stems and lace.

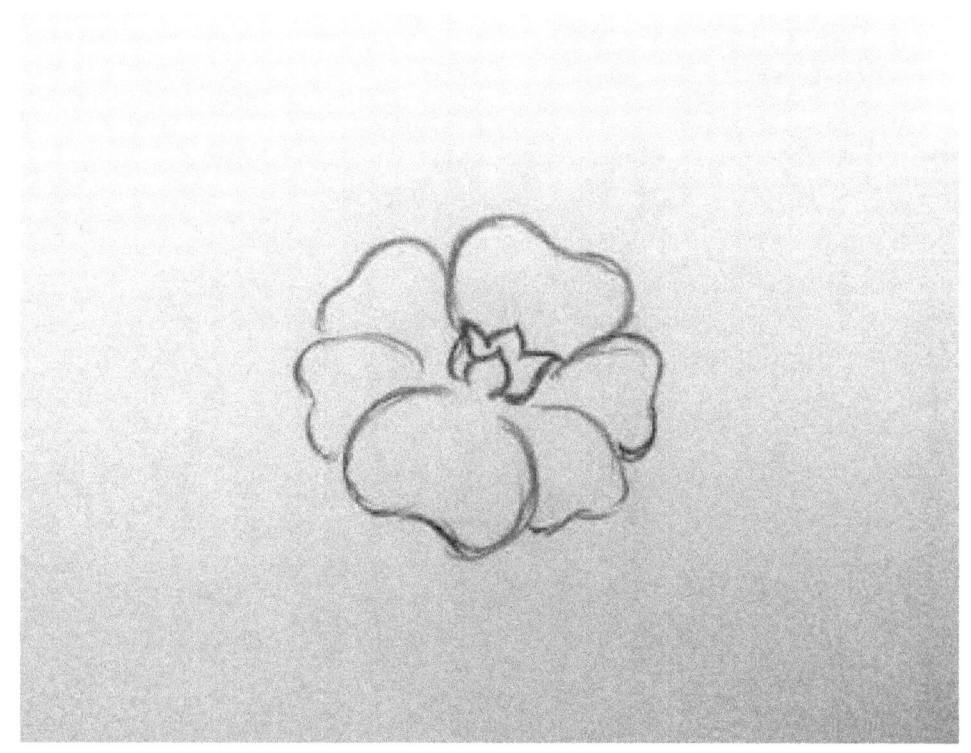

Step 2: Next, start drawing every rose as shut buds. It's least demanding on the off chance that you begin in the inside and move out.

Step 3: Draw in more petals for the roses to make the look of full sprouts. Include the whirls in the focal point of every rose and after that continue to step four.

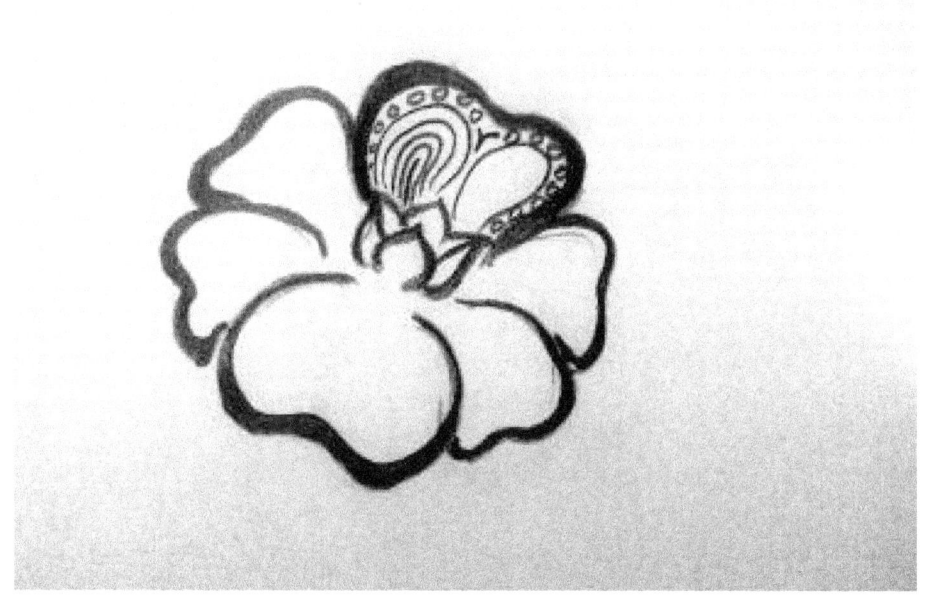

Step 4: The bunch ought to have an assortment of different flowers. So you will draw in basic sprouts that have four petals on every bloom. Draw the leaves and after that add itemizing to the focal point of the clears out.

Step 5: We will now draw in the standard or strip which will show. This can be modified to say anything you like on the off chance that you might want to utilize the instructional exercise for diverse reasons.

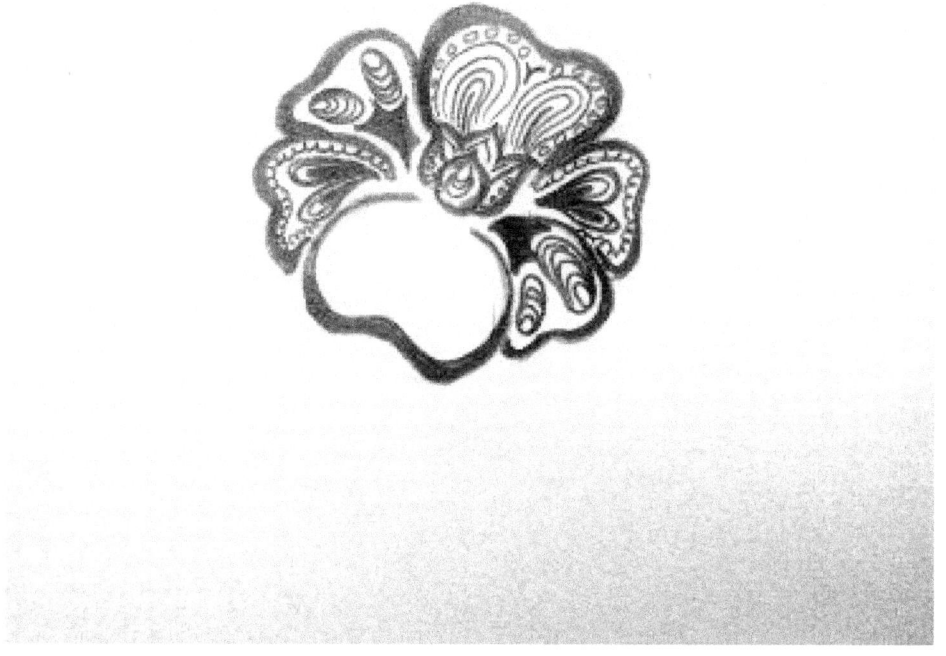

Step 6: Up next, draw in the lovely bow which holds the bunch together. Add specifying to the bow and afterward continue to step seven.

Step 7: In conclusion, we will draw the stems for every one of the flowers and after that draw in the last parts for the strip. Eradicate your slip-ups and you are all done.

Step 8: Here is the line craftsmanship for when you are finished. Presently you can shading in your bunch before you demonstrate the drawing to your mom.

Step 9: Now you can make doodle in the flower and be more creative.

Chapter 2 – How to draw doodle dog

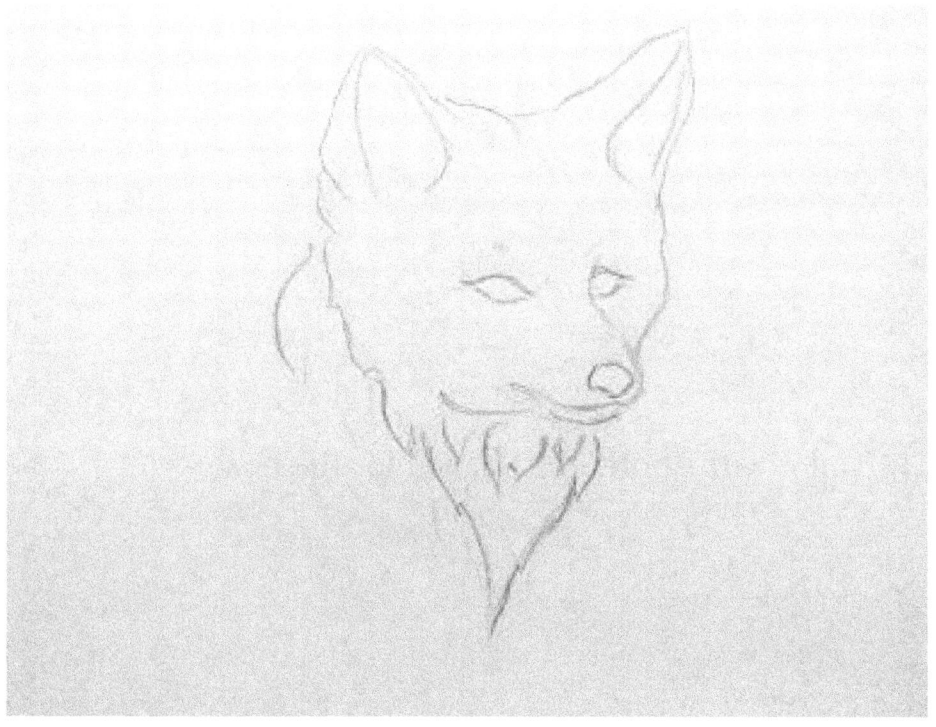

Step 1: Draw a circle.

Step 2: Cover it with an even oval at its base. Make a few twofold lined ovals for the eyes.

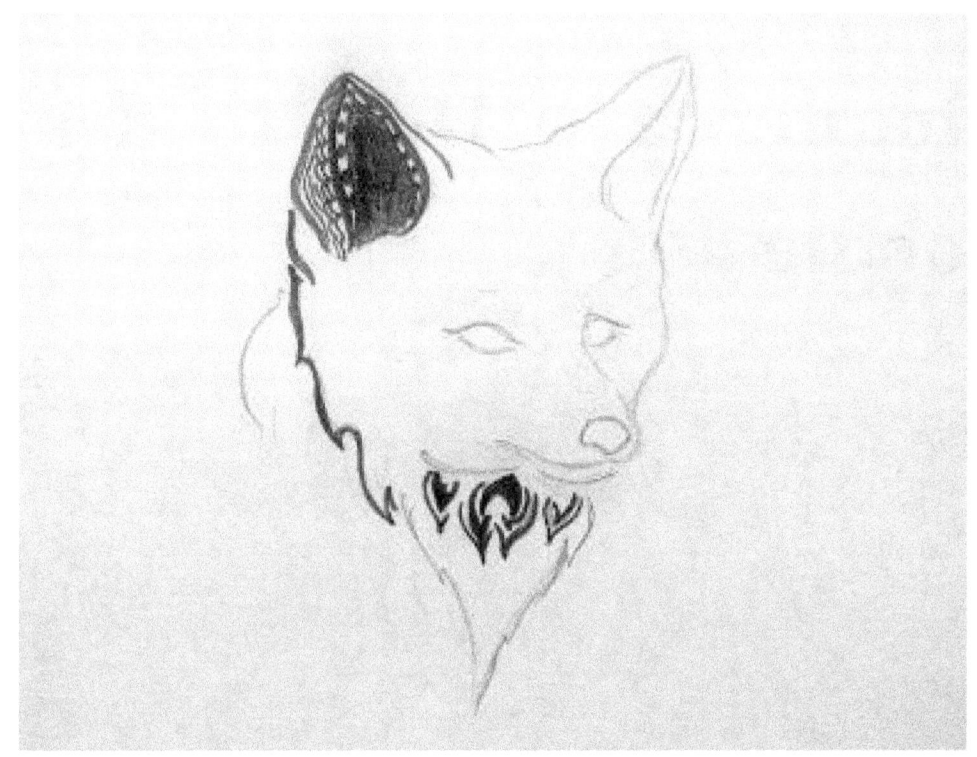

Step 3: Tail it with another little oval for the nose.

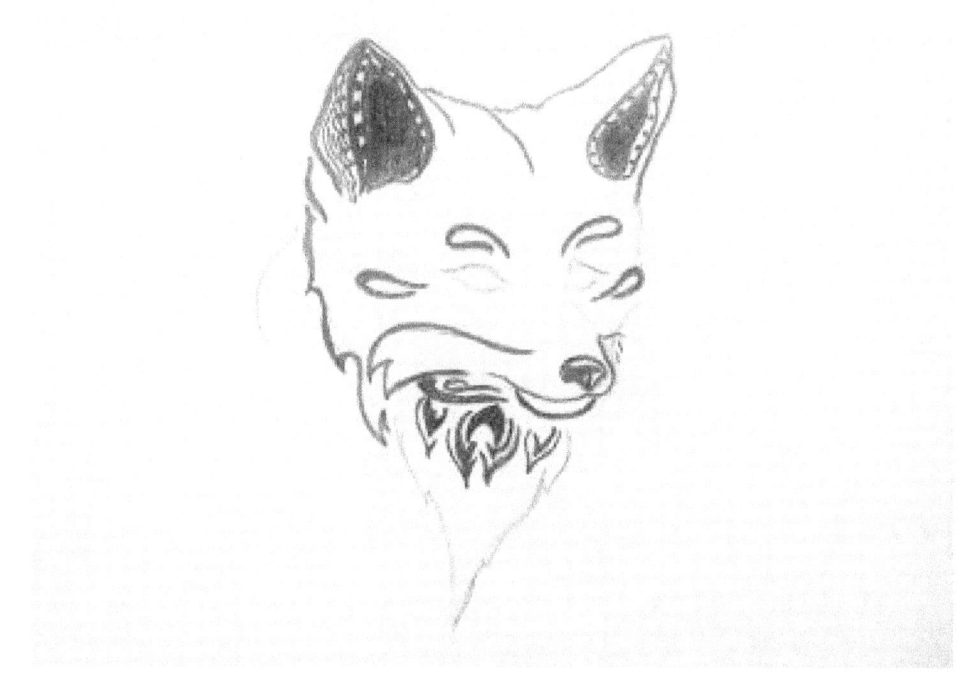

Step 4: Just underneath it draw bended lines for the mouth.

Step 5: Draw one of its ears with bended lines as demonstrated as follows. Correspondingly draw another ear.

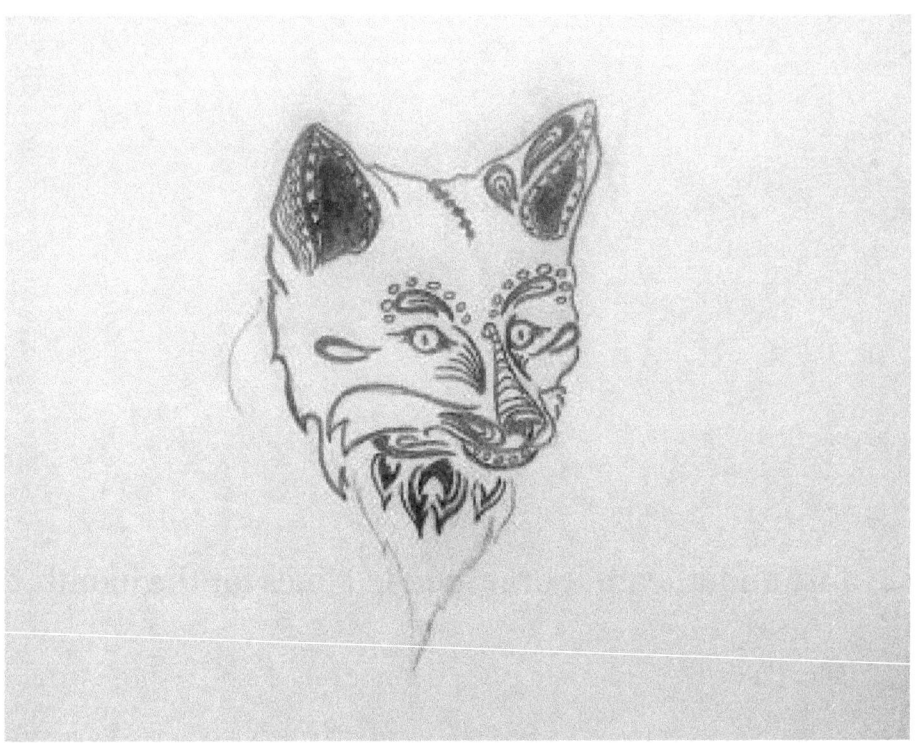

Step 6: Cover the oval at the base with another rectangle. Make and cover the rectangle with a case with bended sides.

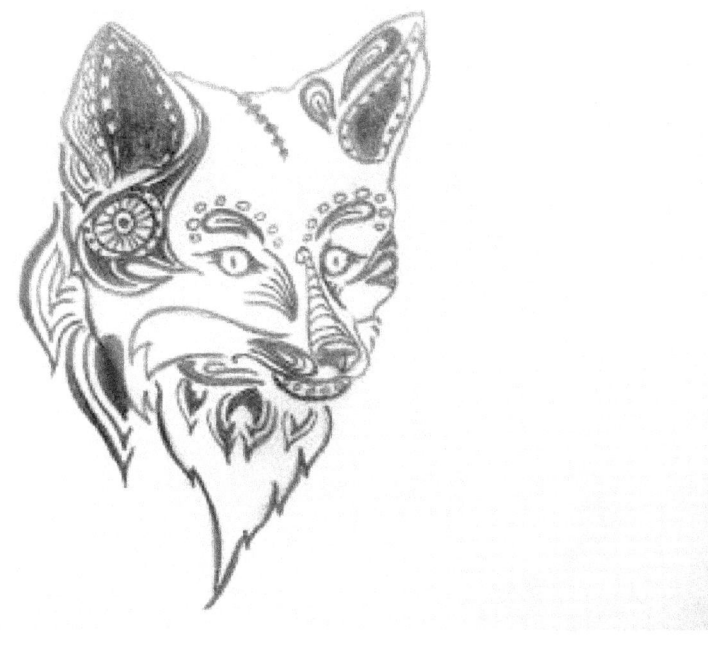

Step 7: Append another covering unpredictable box beneath for the tummy.

Step 8: Cover the base with another sporadic box with bended sides for the lower back.

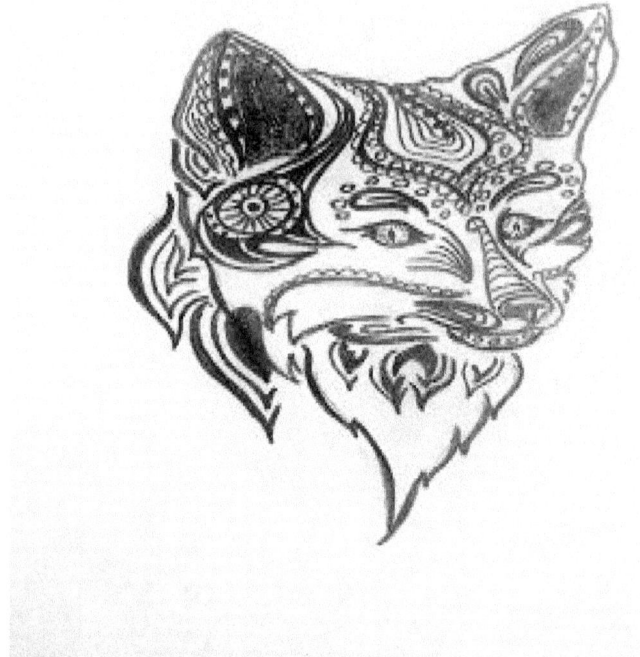

Step 9: Cover a little oval at the base tip for the rear leg paw. Draw a vertical rectangle with bended sides with the upper side open for one of the forelegs.

Step 10: At the base of that rectangle draw covering oval for the foreleg paw.

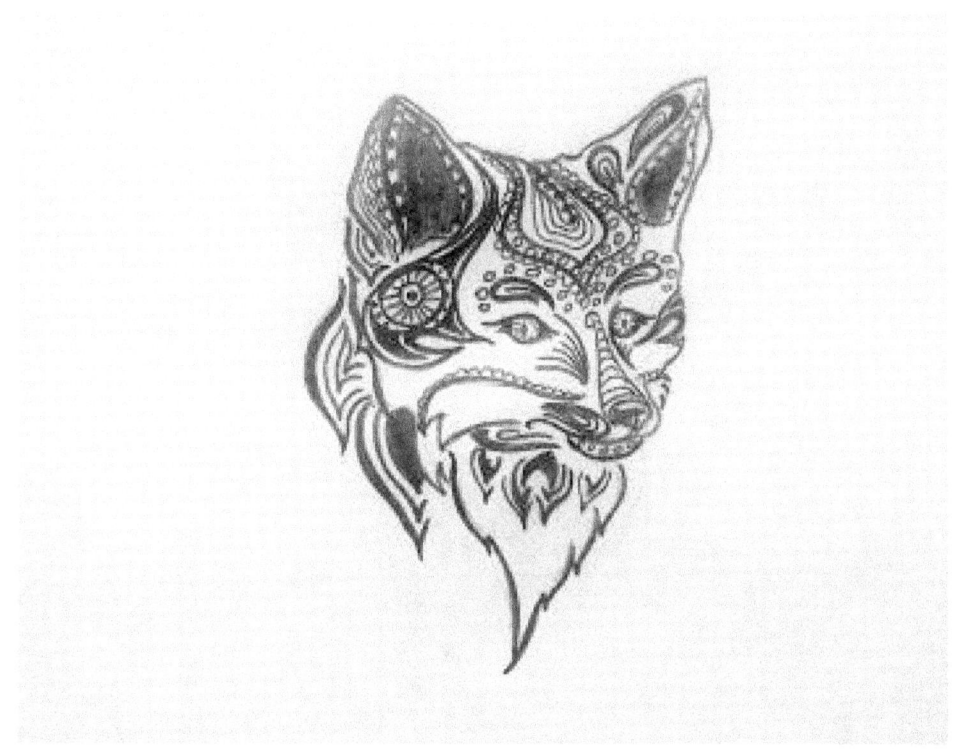

Step 11: Draw a comparable vertical rectangle for another foreleg. Include a little bended line for the tail. Add everything about the drawing taking into account the rules.

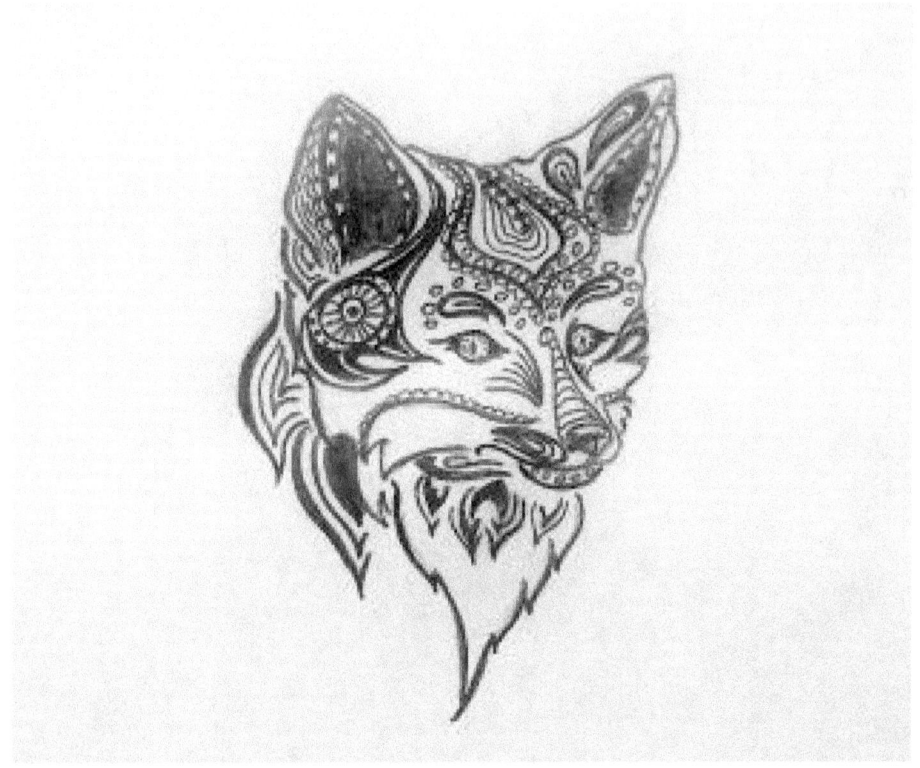

Step 12: Erase all the guidelines.

Chapter 3 – How to draw a cat

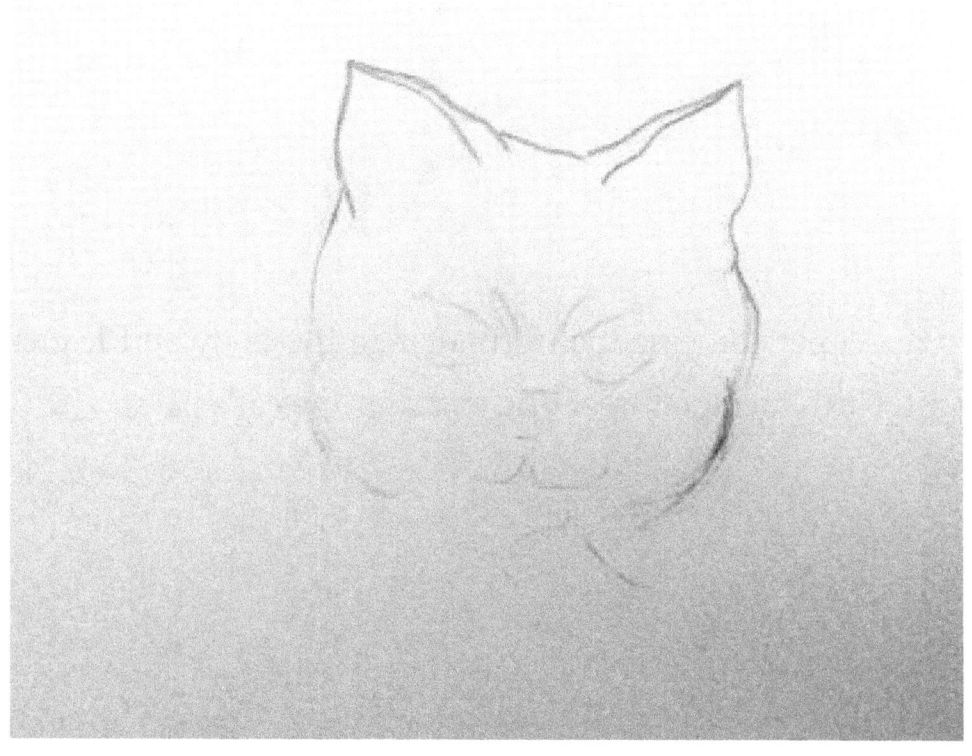

Step 1: Begin with a circle for the state of cat's face and include two circles for the body. Draw two vertical lines at the base for the cat's front legs.

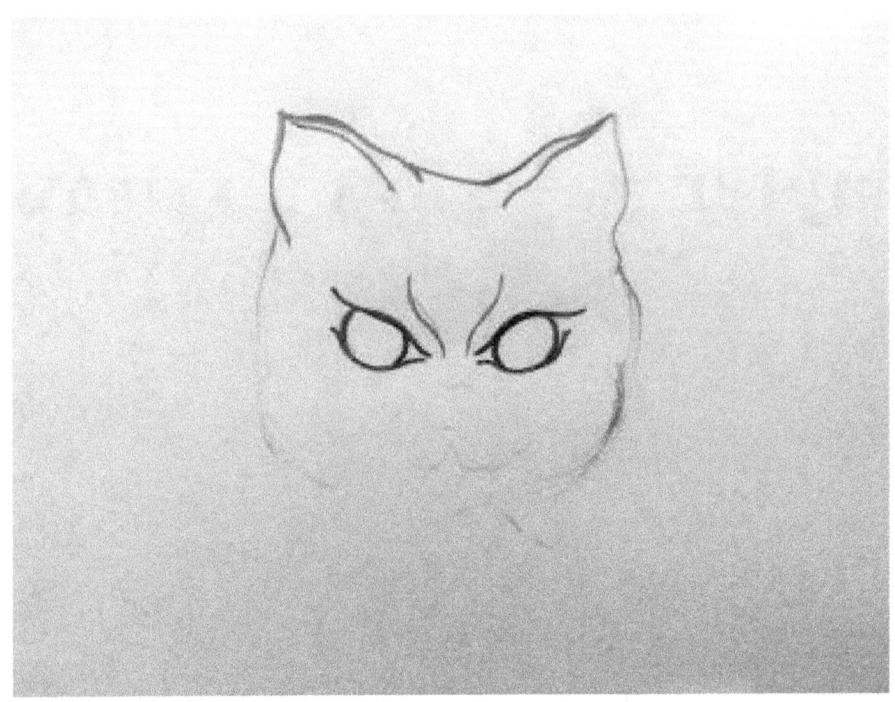

Step 2: As per the essential forms circle the body and leader of the cat. Next, include three little ovals for the cat's paws.

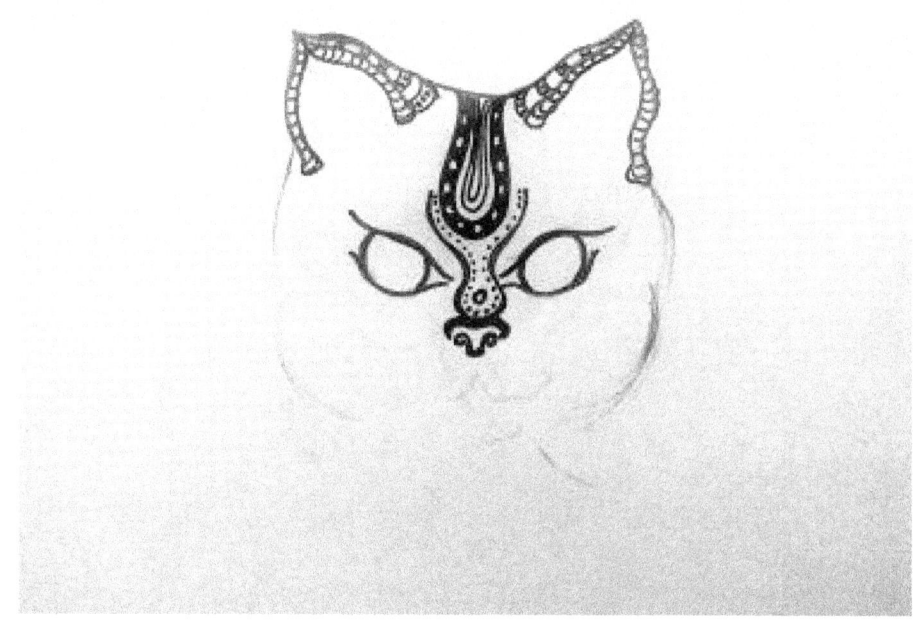

Step 3: Draw the front legs. The cat's legs ought to be the same long and thickness. Subsequent to drawing it, include a starting form (little oval) for the cat's face.

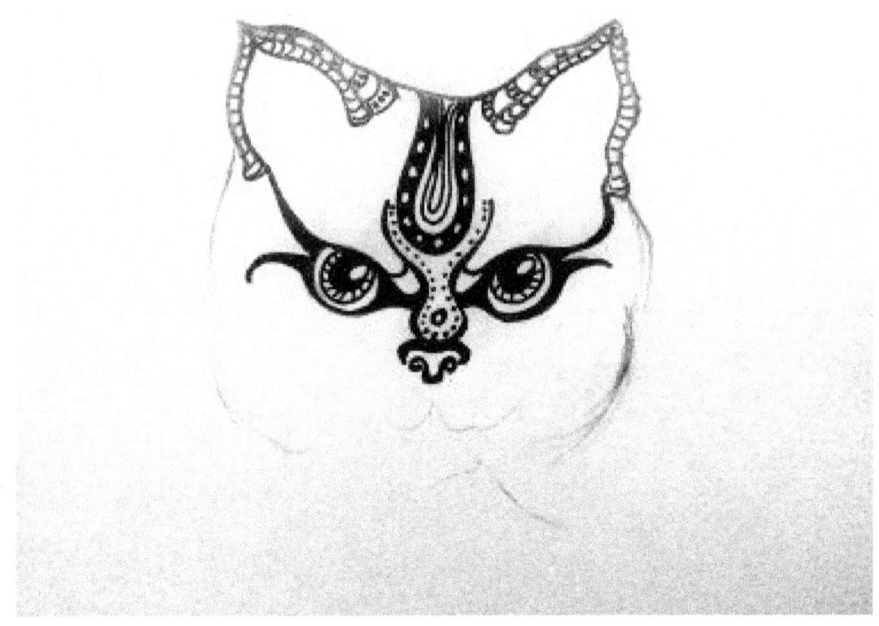

Step 4: Delete every single superfluous line that you attracted the early stages. To complete the sketch, draw the cat's face in subtle element. Draw the gag right - it is the most critical part.

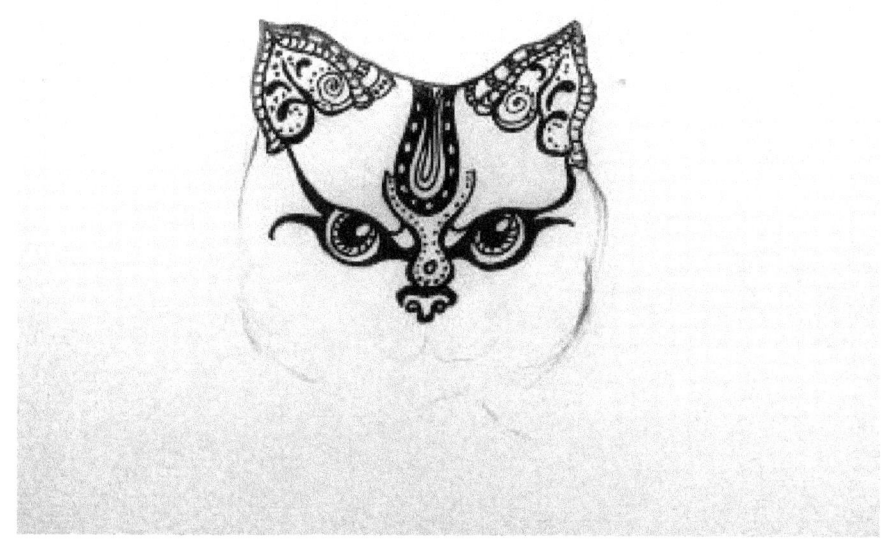

Step 5: Draw the cat's face, as appeared in the figure. Draw eyes, nose and cat's mouth, utilizing the diagram drawn as a part of the past step. Bear in mind to draw the cat's hooks and bristles. After that, you can continue to the last step you're drawing a Cat.

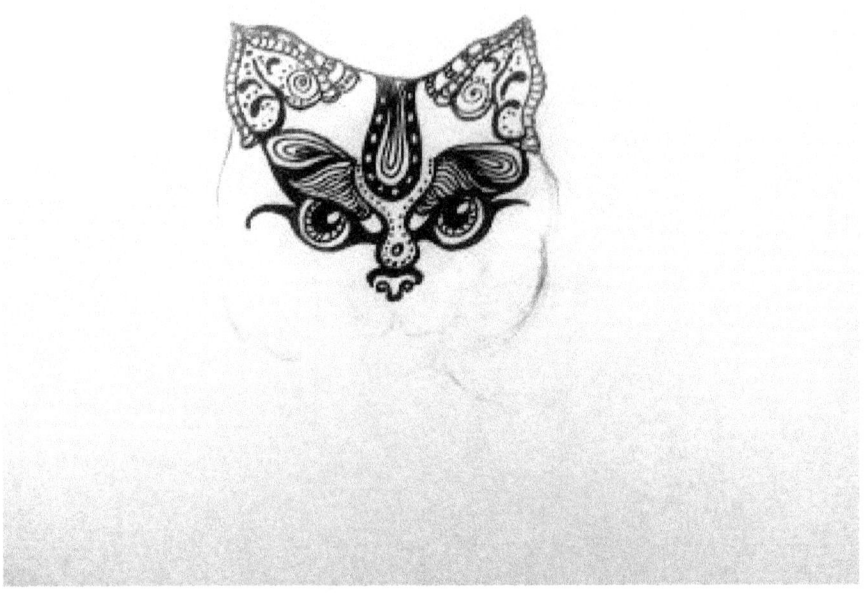

Step 6: Right now, take a shot at the cat's hide. To do this, apply little fast strokes of a pencil on our beginning lines, as appeared on my figure here. Presently, your cat looks practical, you just need to shade in your cat's drawing.

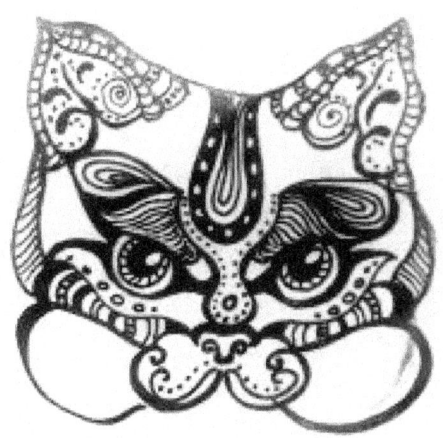

Step 7: Draw the front mid-section of the cat, front legs and back rear leg.

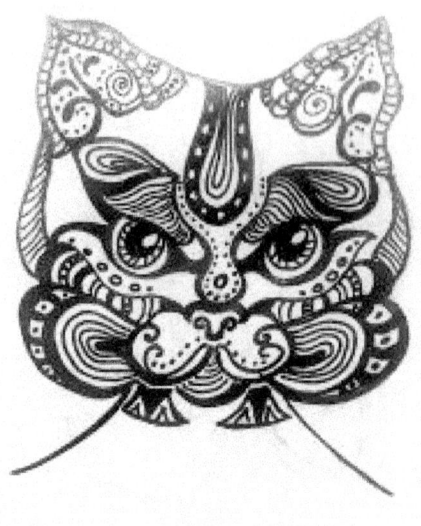

Step 8: Complete the front and back paws of the Cat.

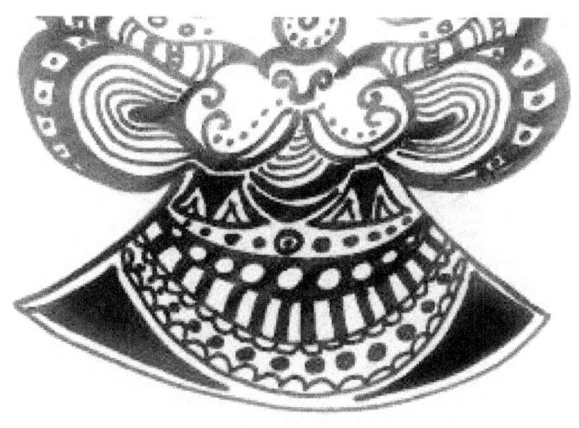

Step 9: Include the Cats tail and you ought to have finished a basic drawing of a Cat sitting on each of the 4 legs.

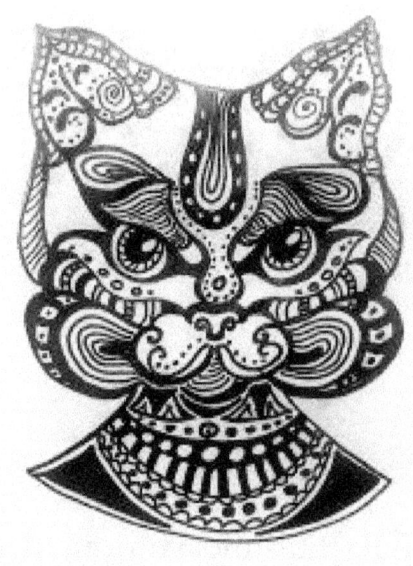

Step 10: Finally erase the guidelines and make sure that you shade the doodle.

Chapter 4 – How to draw a doodle fish

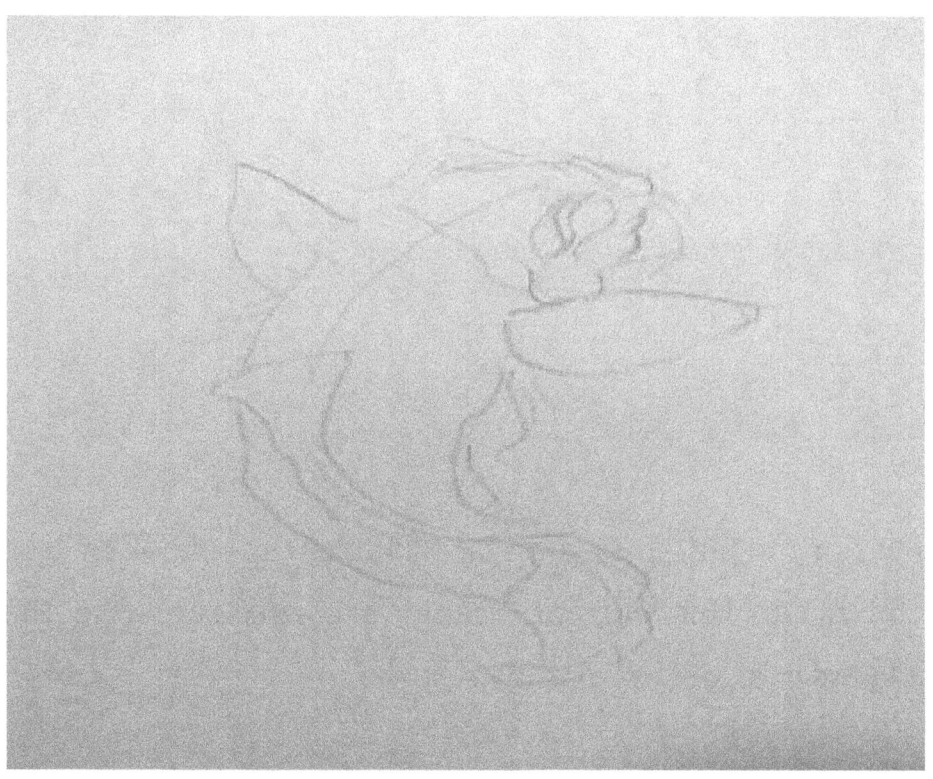

Step 1: Draw a cross rule to adjust our shapes. Draw an oval and a rectangle rule for the fish's body.

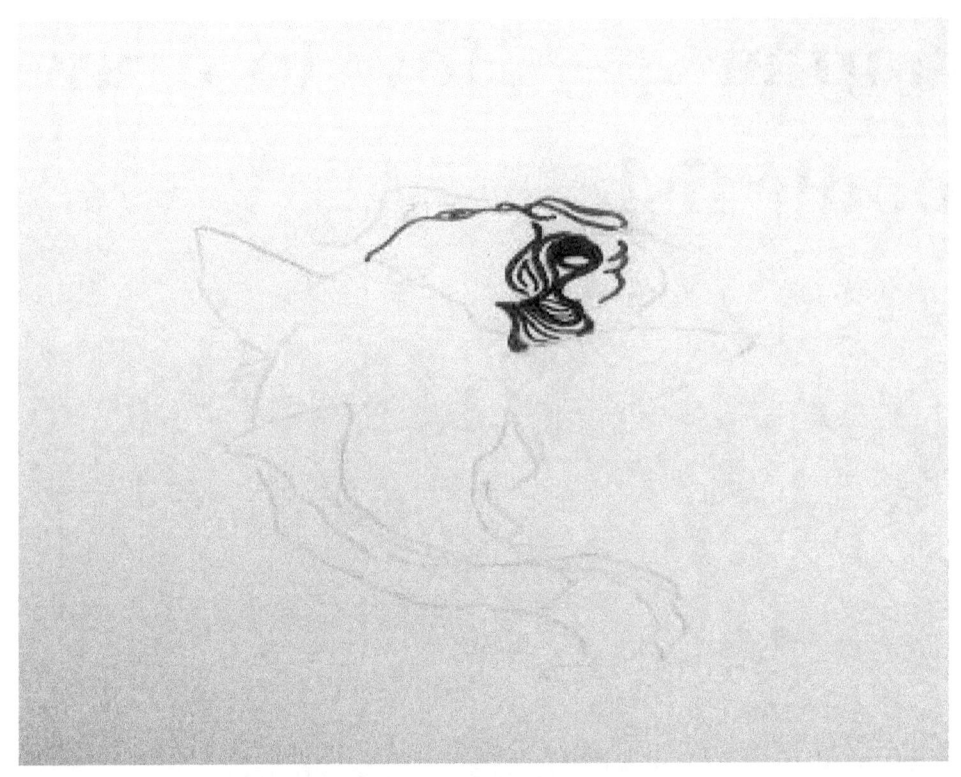

Step 2: For the tail, draw a major triangle. Draw another triangle for the head. This current triangle's corner, the one that is outside the oval, decreases downwards.

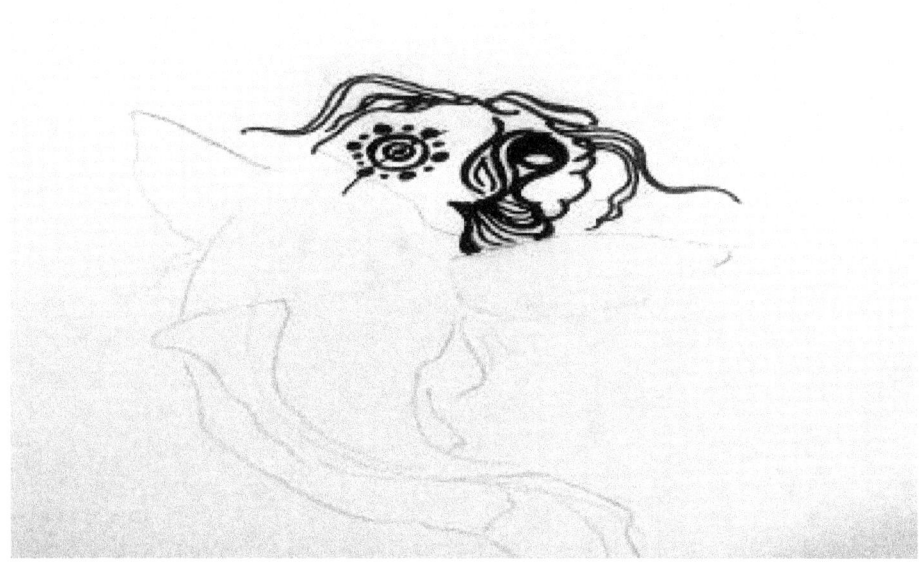

Step 3: Layout the last state of the fish utilizing the rules. Draw the mouth like a retrogressive 3. The edge of the tail is drawn with a wavy line bending inwards the extensive triangle rule. Draw the gill spread with 2 curves. Finally, draw a circle for the eyes.

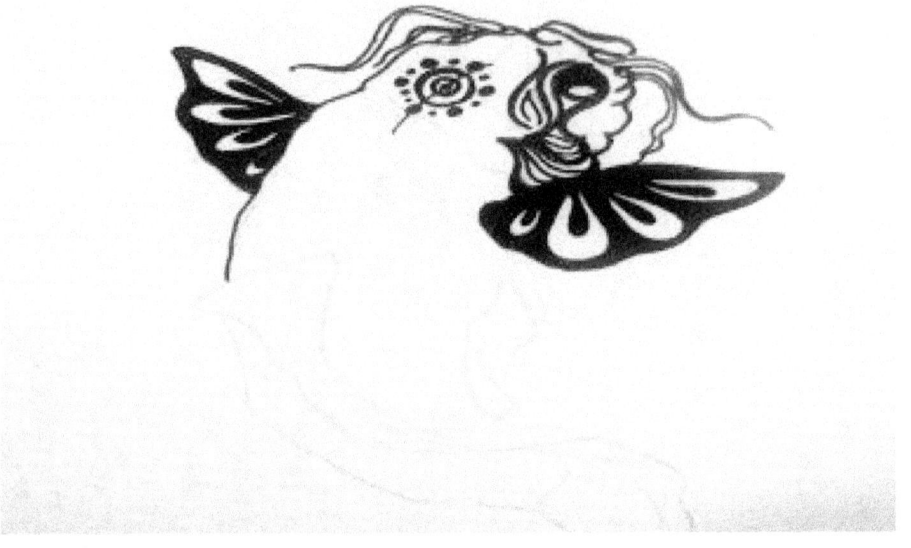

Step 4: Delete the rules totally. Draw the dorsal balances with a wavy line. Draw one balance close to the gill spread and the other balance near the base edge of the fish.

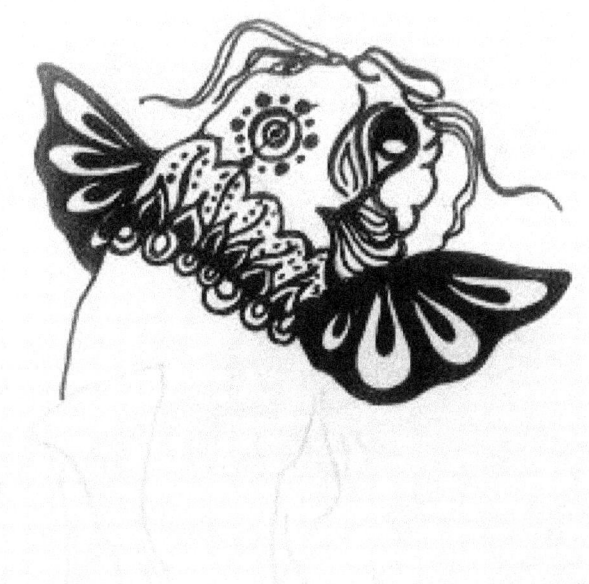

Step 5: These balances ought to appear to be like an unpredictable thin V.

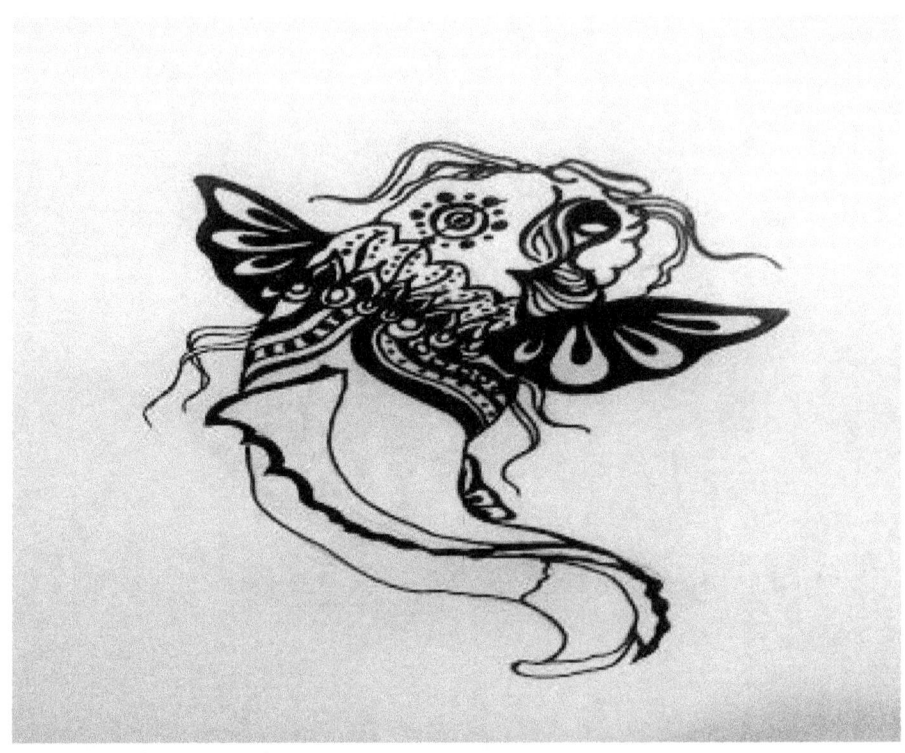

Step 6: Eradicate the lines inside the balances and draw a circle for the fish's student.

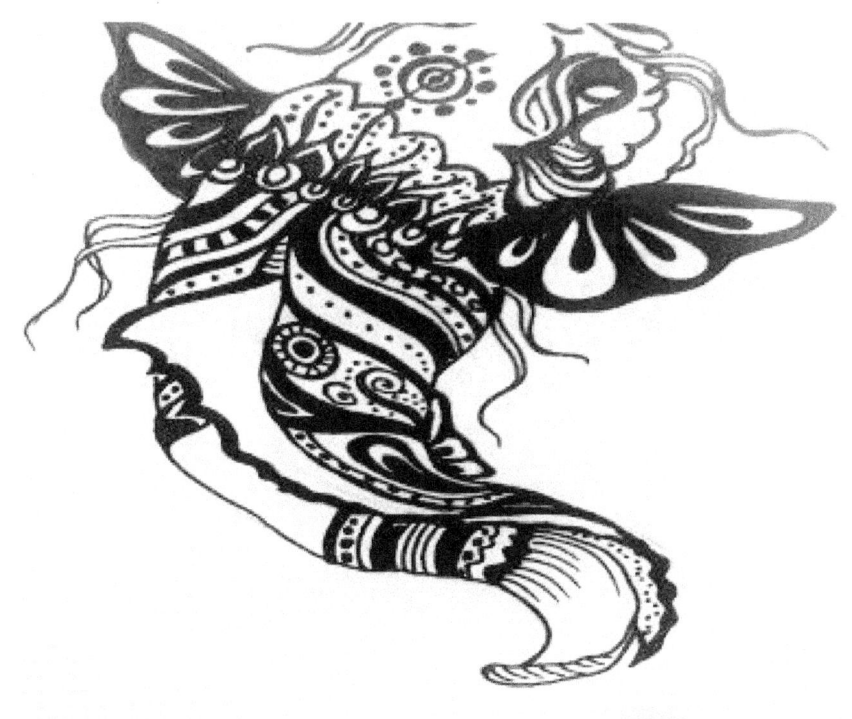

Step 7: Detail the internal parts of the balances and tail by drawing wavy lines.

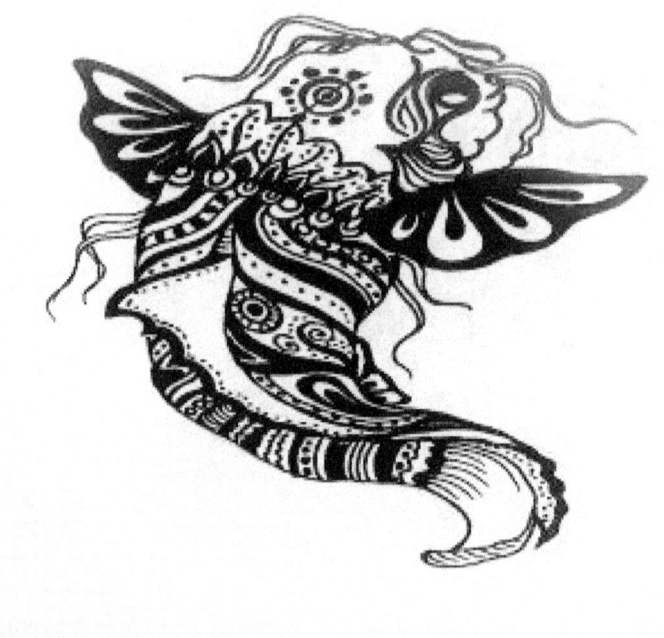

Step 8: Detail the body of the fish by drawing scales. Draw little in reverse C's inside the fish's body to make the scales.

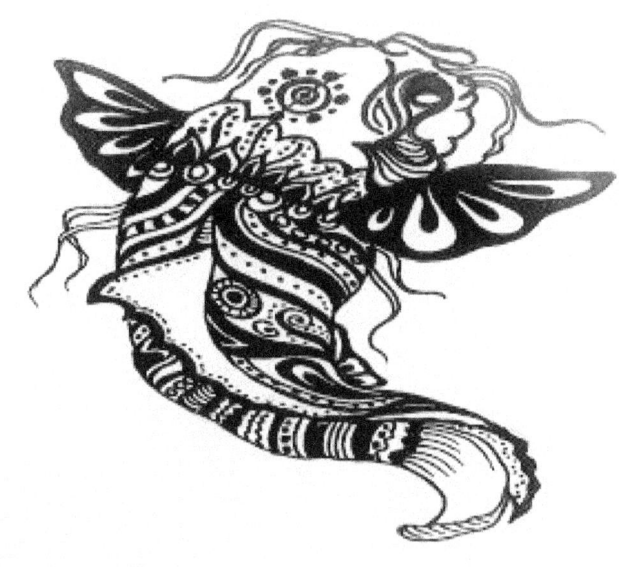

Step 9: Now you can make doodle easier to be seen on the fish, and draw different patterns.

Chapter 5 – How to draw doodle flower

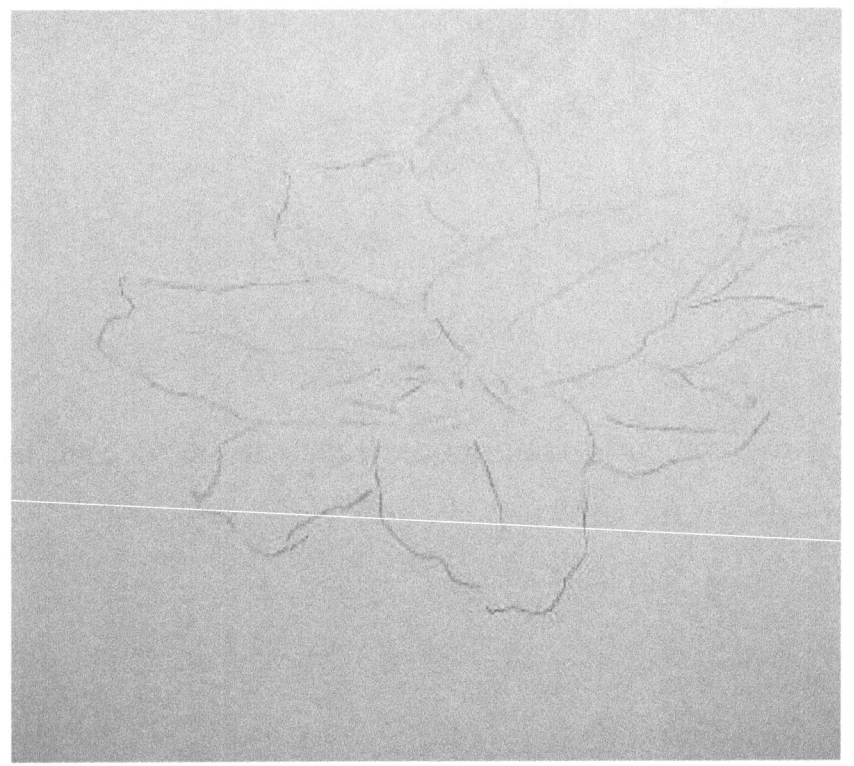

Step 1: Make one circle to frame the inside fringe of the flower.

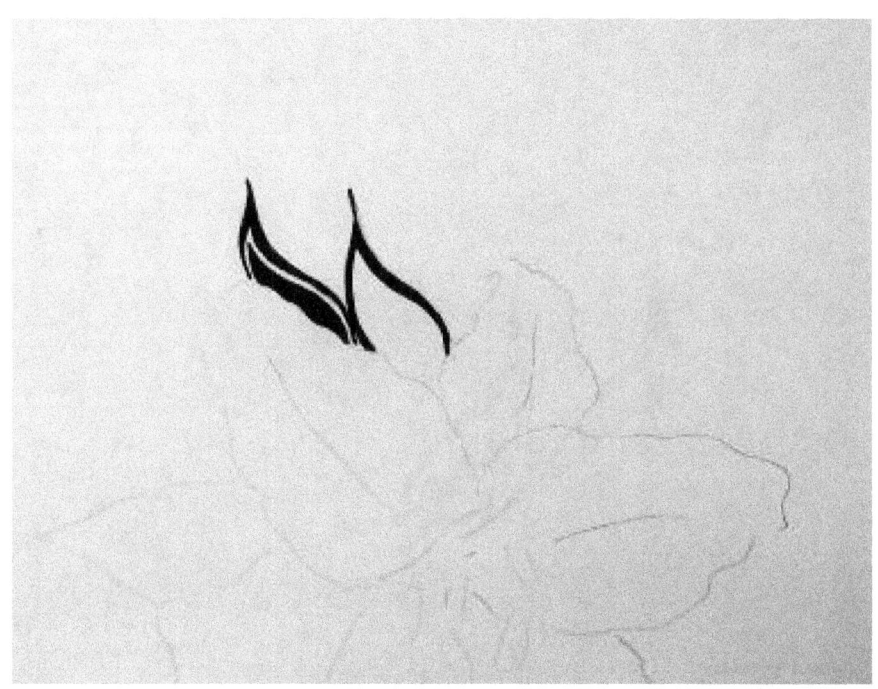

Step 2: Add two more circles to frame the external fringe of the flower petals. Draw the doodle patterns in each and every leaf of the flower.

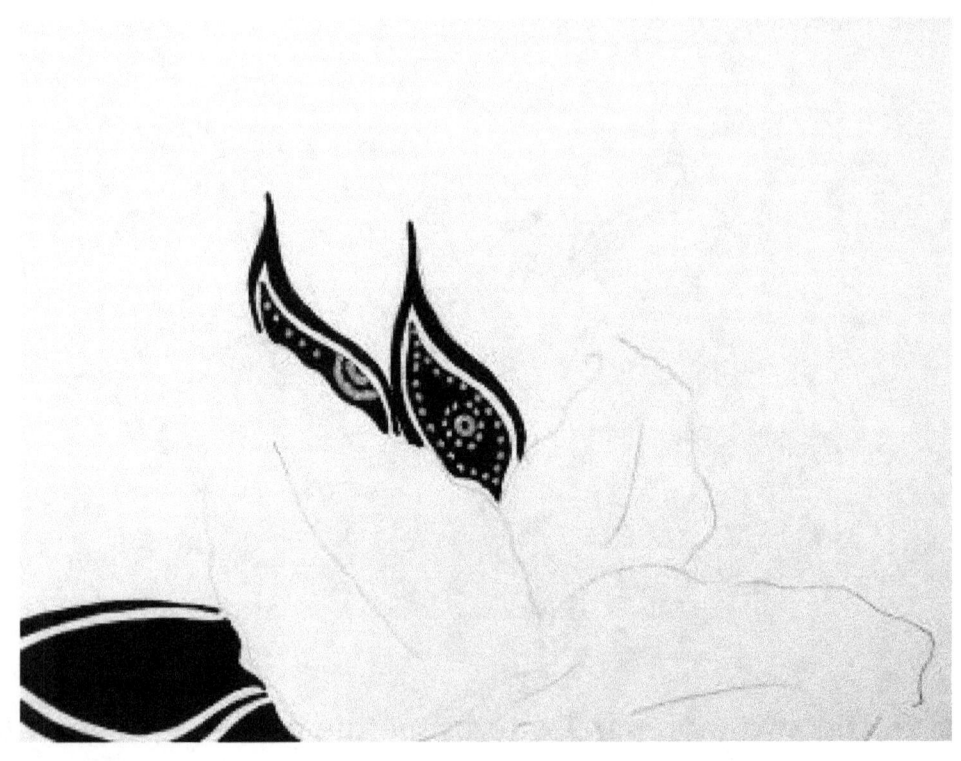

Step 3: Add some harsh structures for the petals.

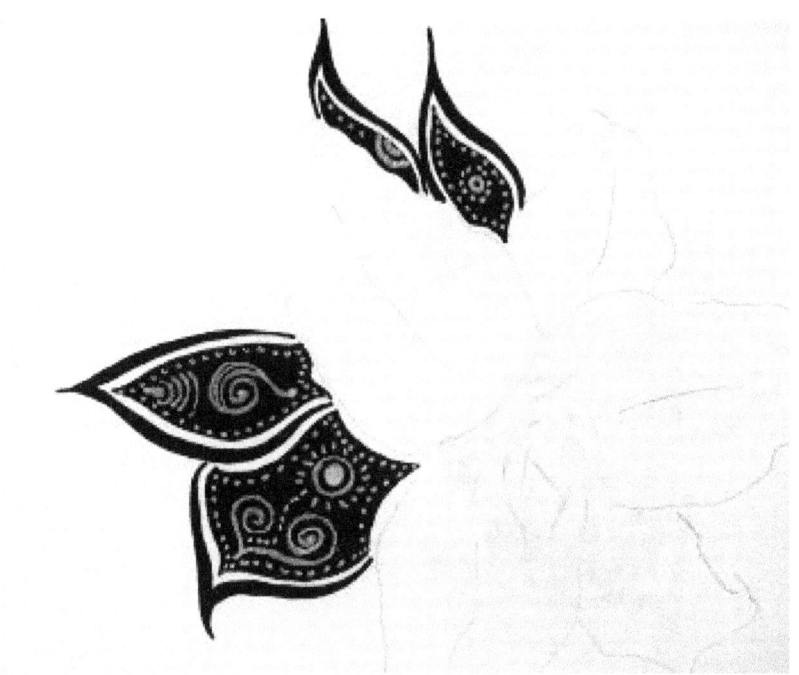

Step 4: Draw the last lines.

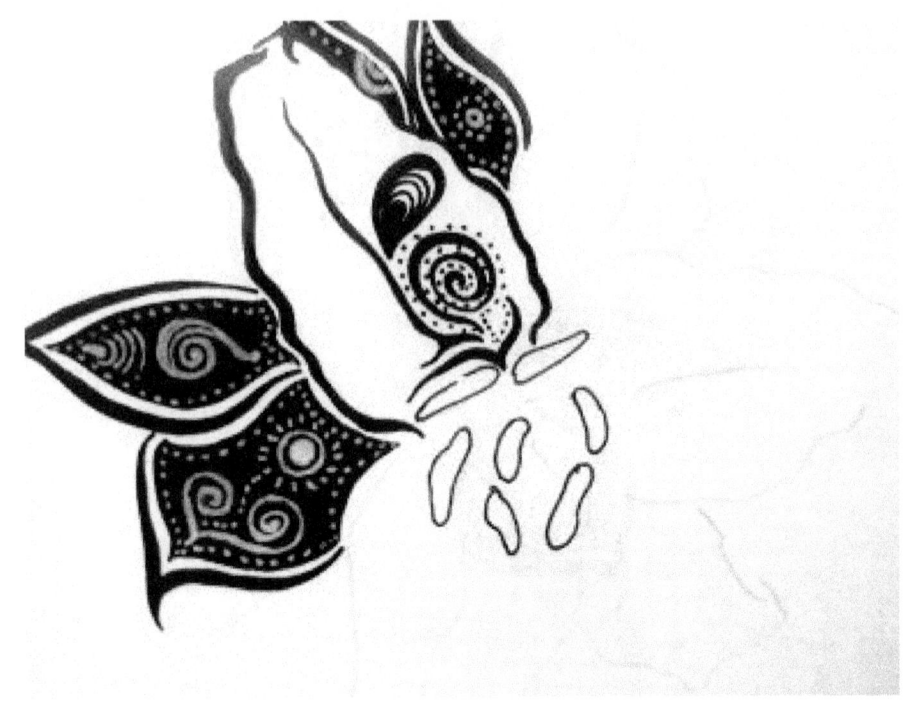

Step 5: Color the drawing and include a few shadows and definition lines.

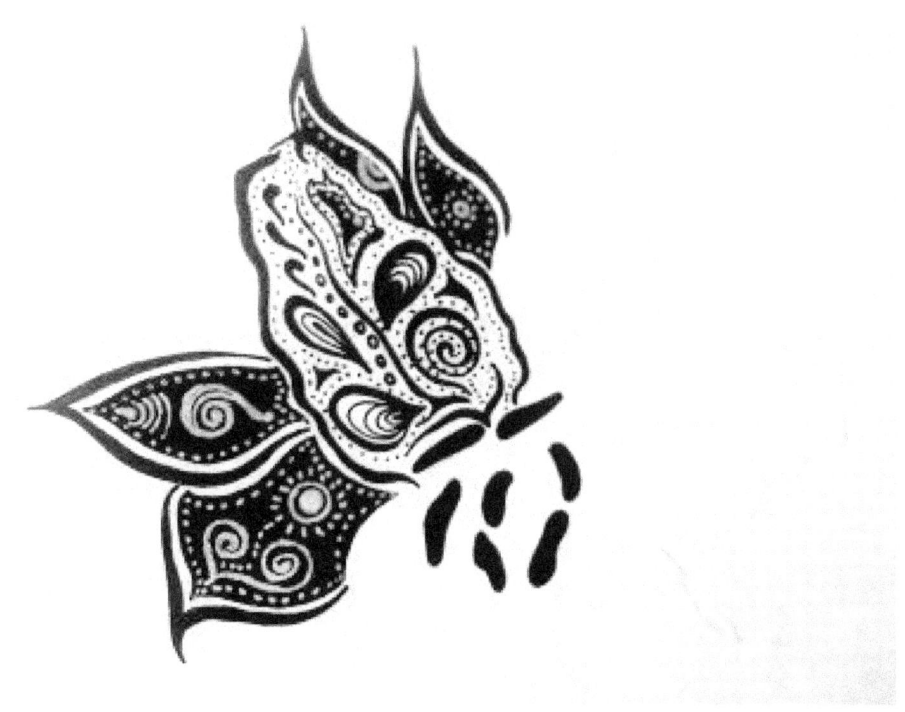

Step 6: Draw an oval to frame the external edge of the flower leaves. Include two parallel lines and join the parallel lines at base as appeared in the photo. Draw different patterns in each and every leaf.

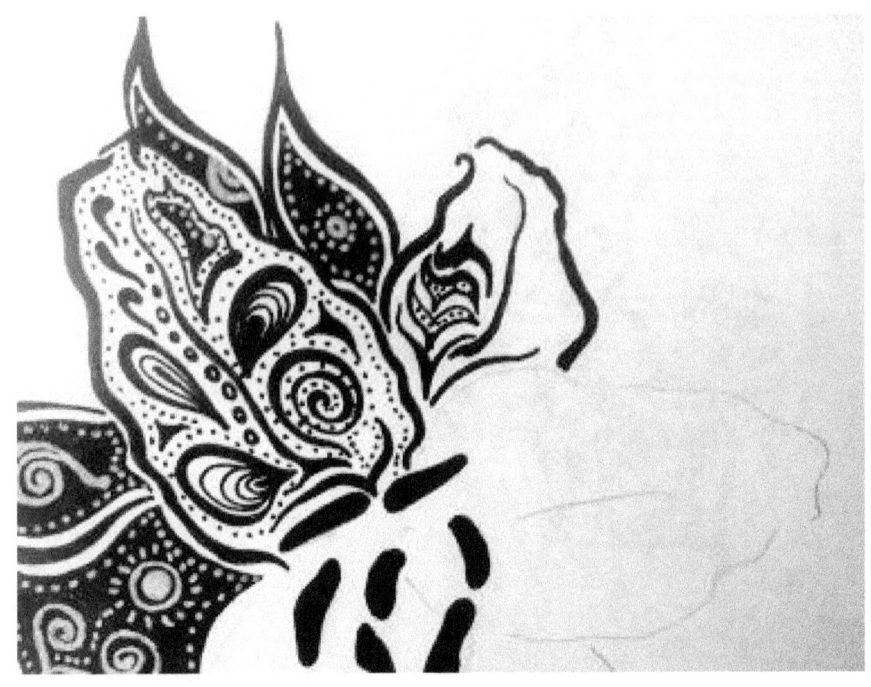

Step 7: Draw an associating littler oval figure at the highest point of the parallel lines to shape the highest point of the flower.

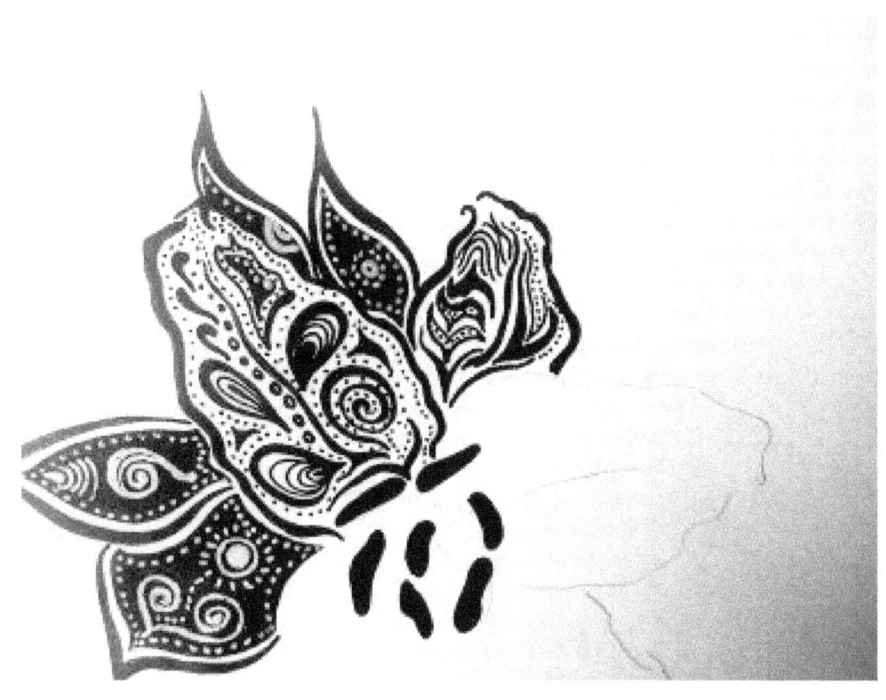

Step 8: Sketch the petals encompassing the greater circle. They ought to be practically of the same sizes and shape.

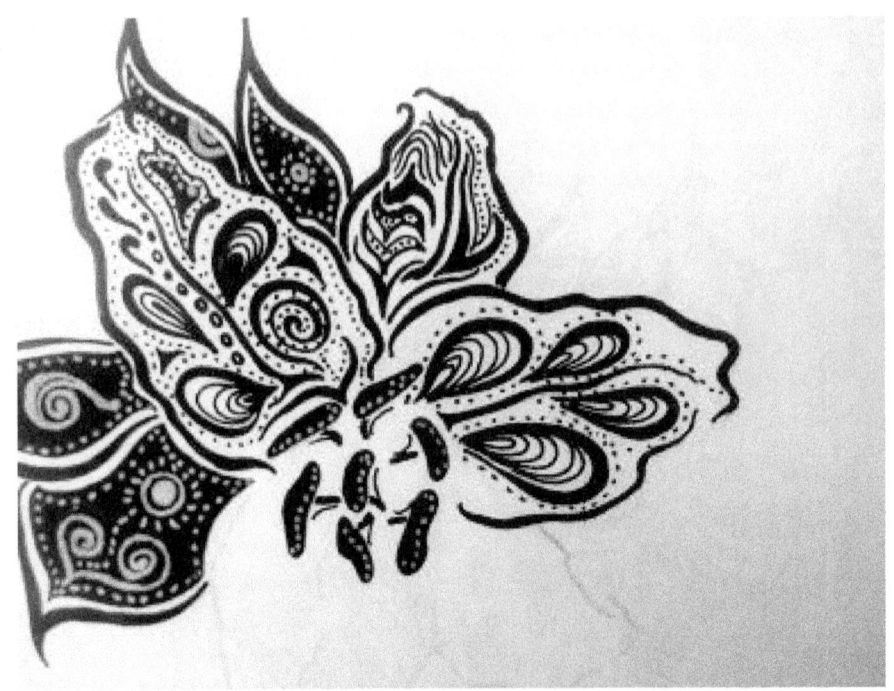

Step 9: Draw semi-circles around the littler circle subsequently, making a flower-like structure. At that point you could include something in the center.

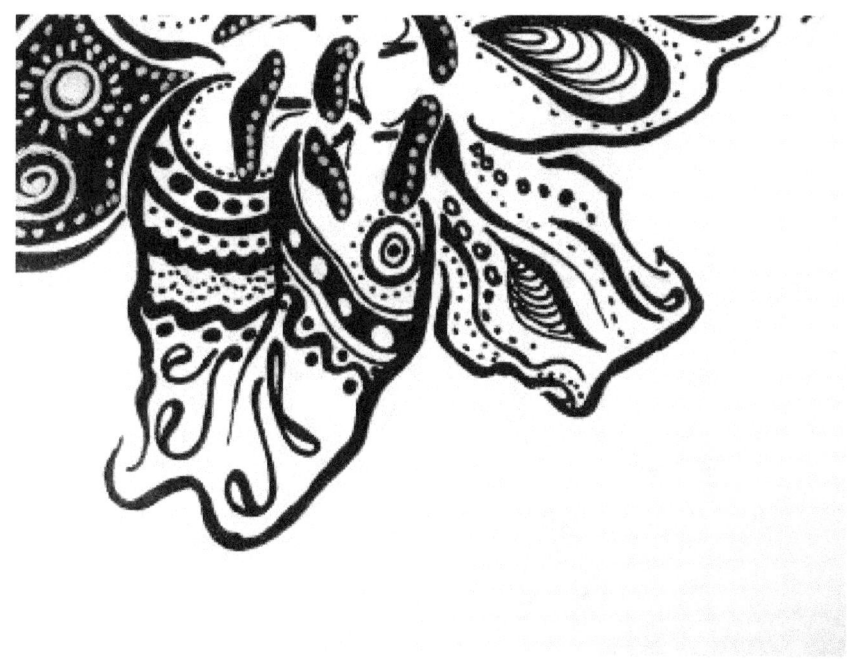

Step 10: Draw the fundamental layout of the petals. The petals at the front ought to be separated from the petals at the back.

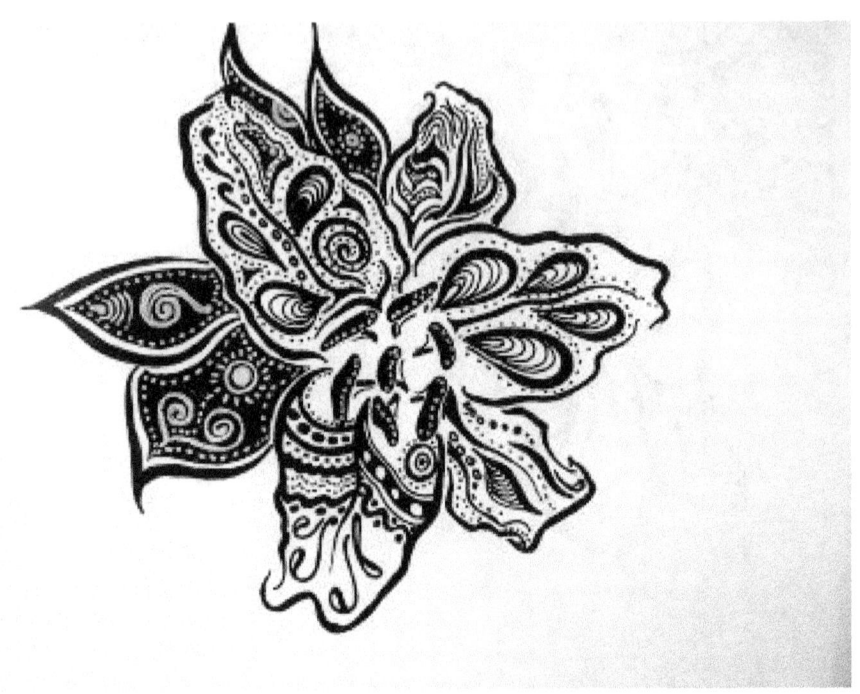

Step 11: Draw the diagram of the greater circle and the stalk. Include more details.

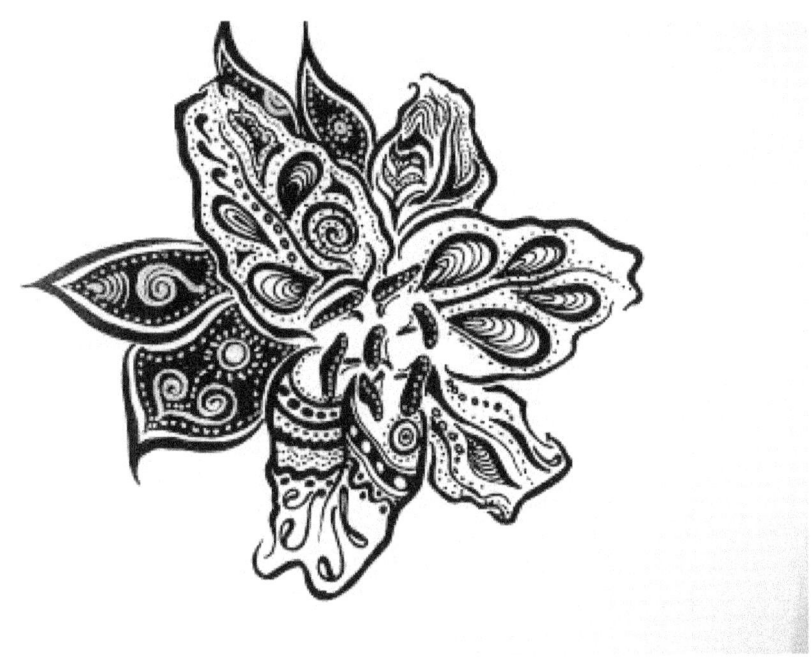

Step 12: Draw and finalize the patterns in the leaf.

Chapter 6 – How to draw a doodle skull

Step 1: Begin by making a basic circle shape for the skull's head and after that draw another aide shape for the jaw.

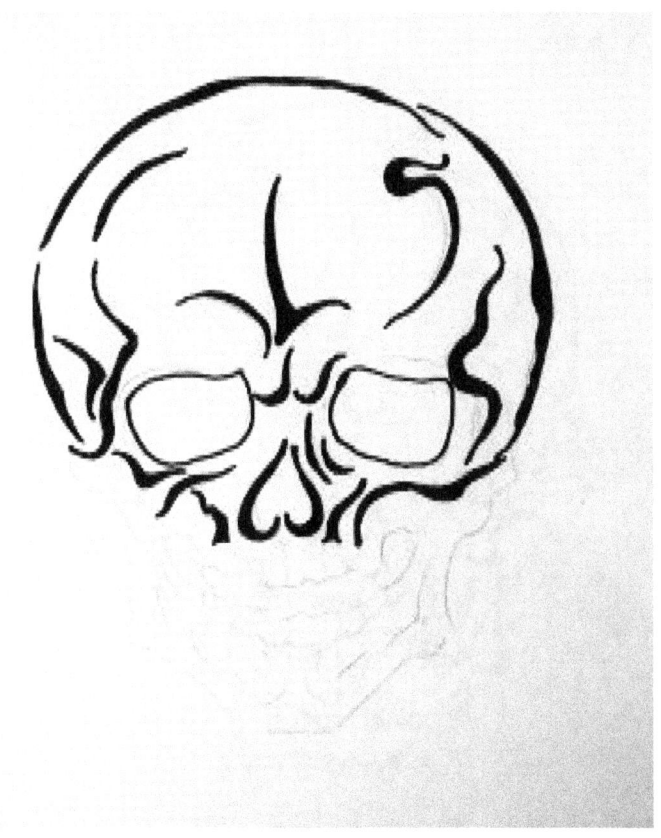

Step 2: Next, start sketching out the hard cheek bone on the privilege and afterward draw in the side perspective of the nose or nasal region. Beneath that shape is the top a portion of the skull's mouth.

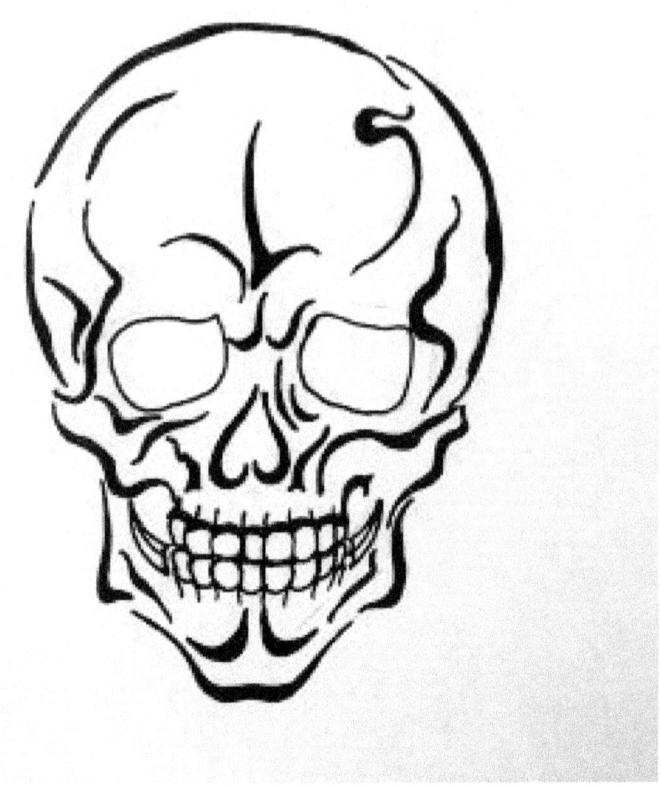

Step 3: Define the state of the skull's head like in this way, then start sketching in the inverse cheek bone alongside whatever remains of the top part of the mouth. Draw in the curves for every tooth too.

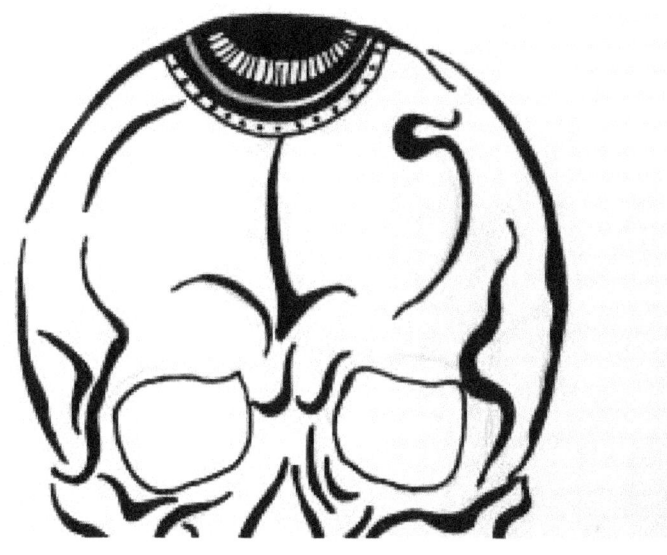

Step 4: We can now draw in the teeth and for me I needed them pointed. When you are finished with the mouth make an expansive circle for the eye empty.

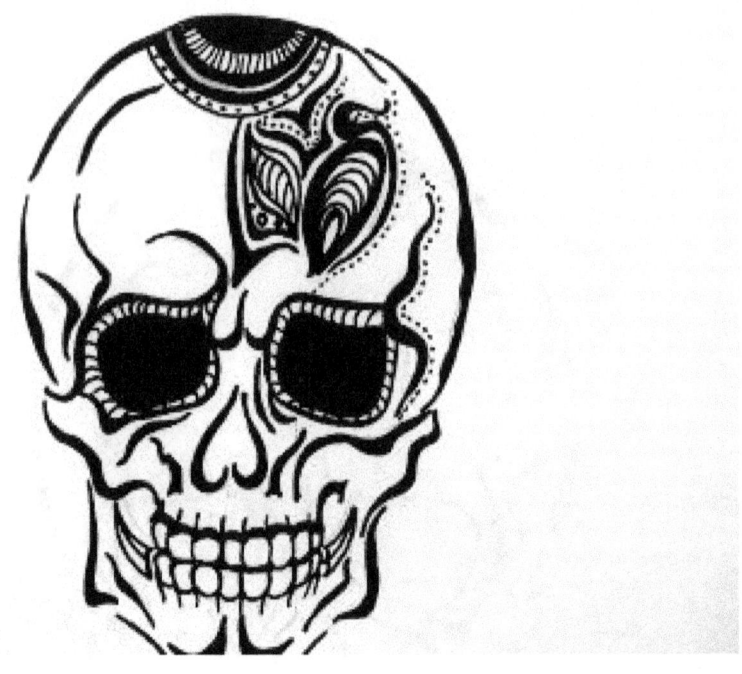

Step 5: This is the last step and with this specific lesson it's a smart thought to eradicate your rules and slip-ups. It's a smart thought to do this in light of the fact that you should shading in the eye empty and the nasal empty.

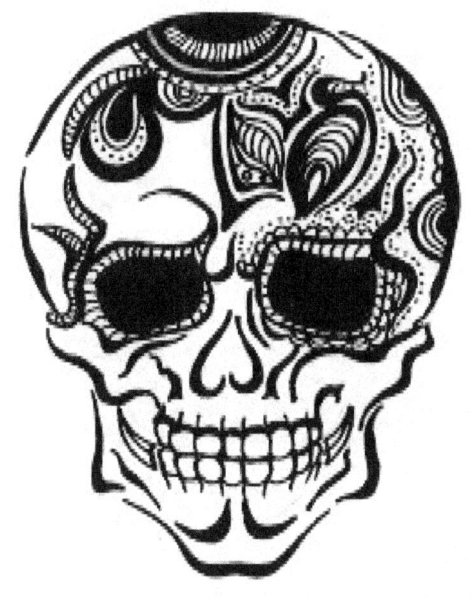

Step 6: In this stride all you will need to do is start using so as to frame the head shape the aide you simply made, then draw the detailed structure of the hard cheeks.

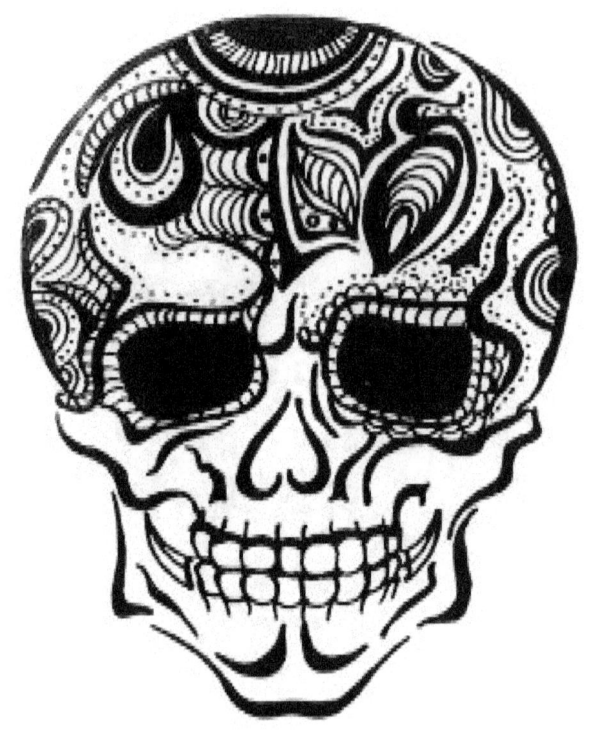

Step 7: In this next step how about we sketch out the screwy shapes for every eye attachment like along these lines, then draw in the nasal depression. Ensure there are scores on the sides of the nose coating to give this rotting skull age. Likewise sketch in a few wrinkles and definition around the eyes and under the nose.

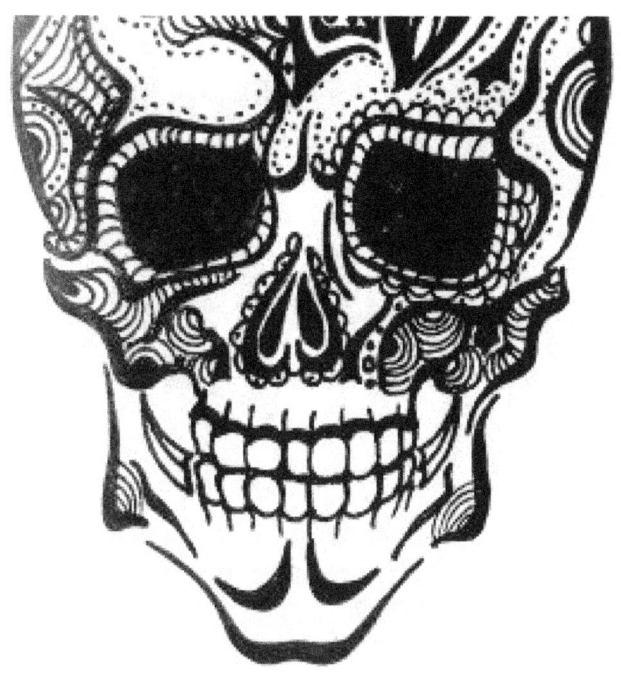

Step 8: You will now draw in the top some portion of the mouth took after by the warped, matured teeth.

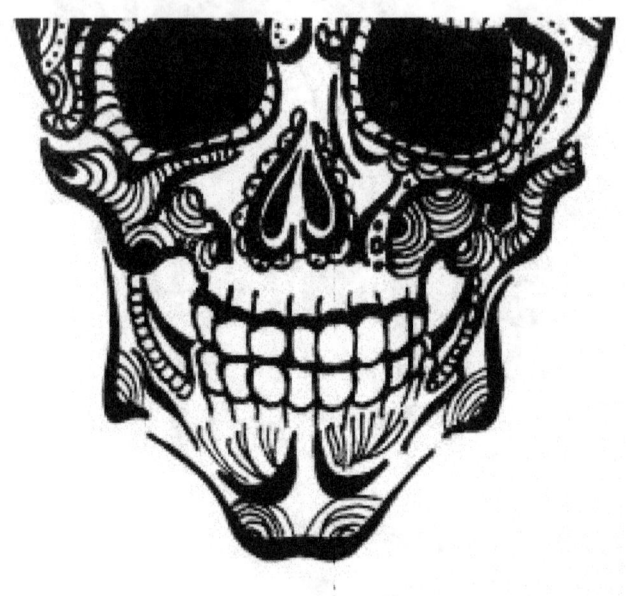

Step 9: Up next, draw in the thick lower some portion of the mouth which is the jaw structure, button and teeth. Add detailing to the side of the jaw as well. The base teeth are slanted and matured too.

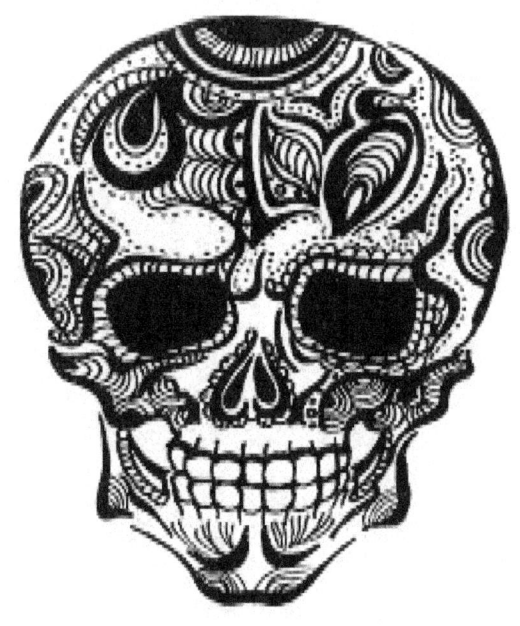

Step 10: For the last step you should simply draw in the straggly bits of hair and every one of the breaks, roots or veins and the dimpling over the top line of teeth. Eradicate every one of the errors and you are good to go.

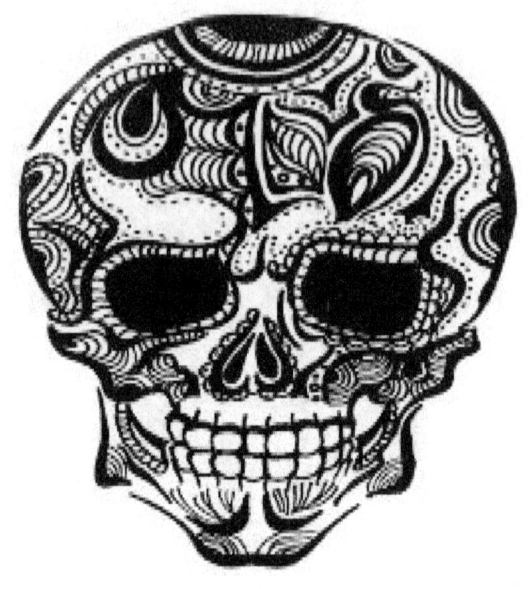

Step 11: Here is the line workmanship for your new drawing when you are finished. Presently you can simply ahead and shading everything in.

Chapter 7 – How to draw a doodle fish

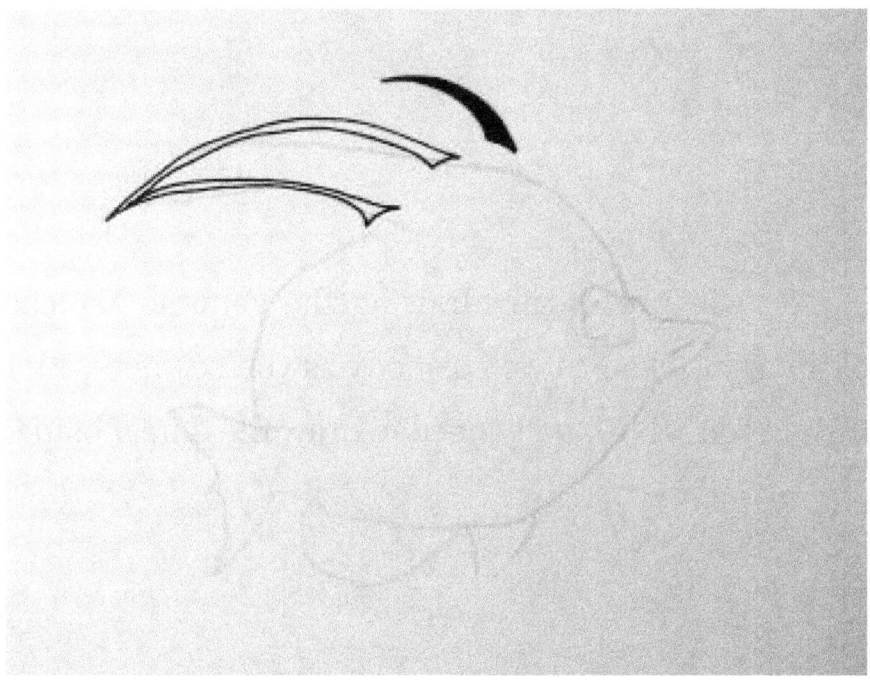

Step 1: Drawing a fish will be simple for all of you in light of the fact that you will be learning from Dragoart.com. Begin with a circle shape for the fish's head and after that include the facial rules. Next draw a little triangular shape for the back end of the fish, and afterward draw the covering for the tail balance, and pelvic fins.

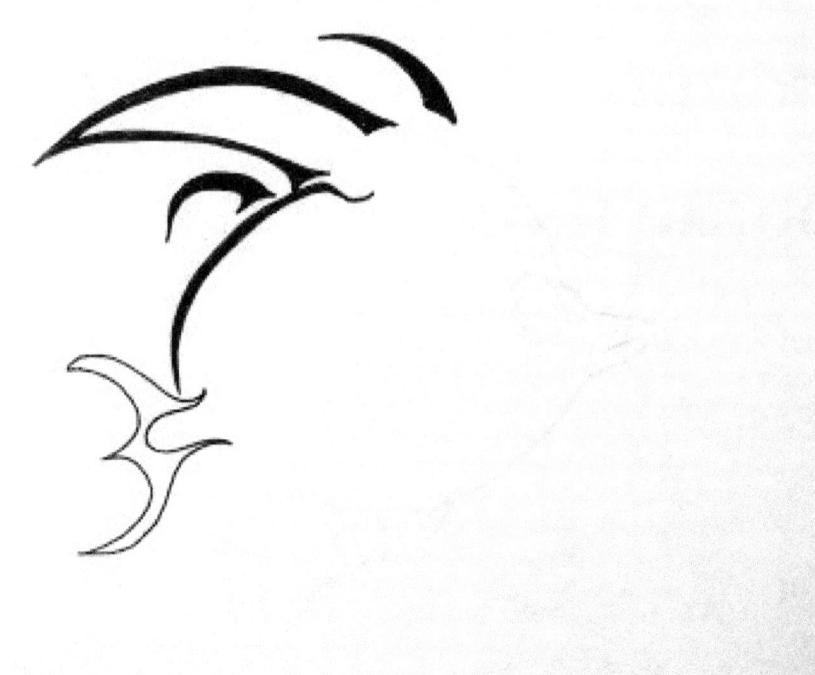

Step 2: You will now begin drawing the genuine sketched out state of the fish's head as well as body as you see here. Alongside the covering you additionally need to draw the dorsal blade.

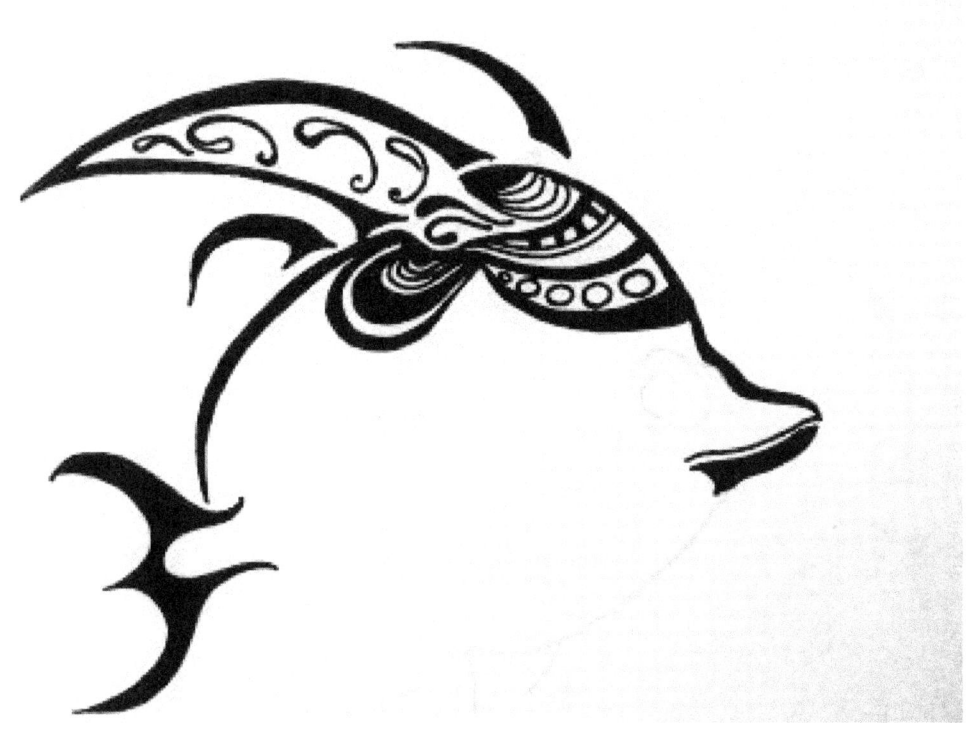

Step 3: Almost done folks! Complete the process of sketching out the body including the tail blade, and pelvic fins, and afterward draw in a charming little sort of mouth.

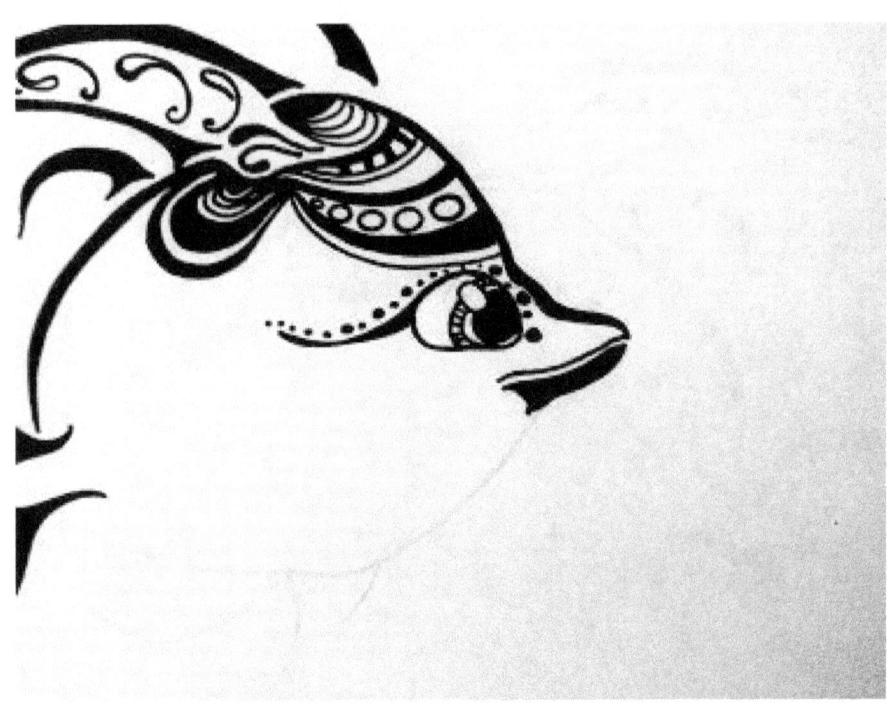

Step 4: Lastly, draw out and shading in the eyes, and after that include some adding so as to detail for the fins, and surface definition a couple scales like you see here. Delete every one of the lines and shapes.

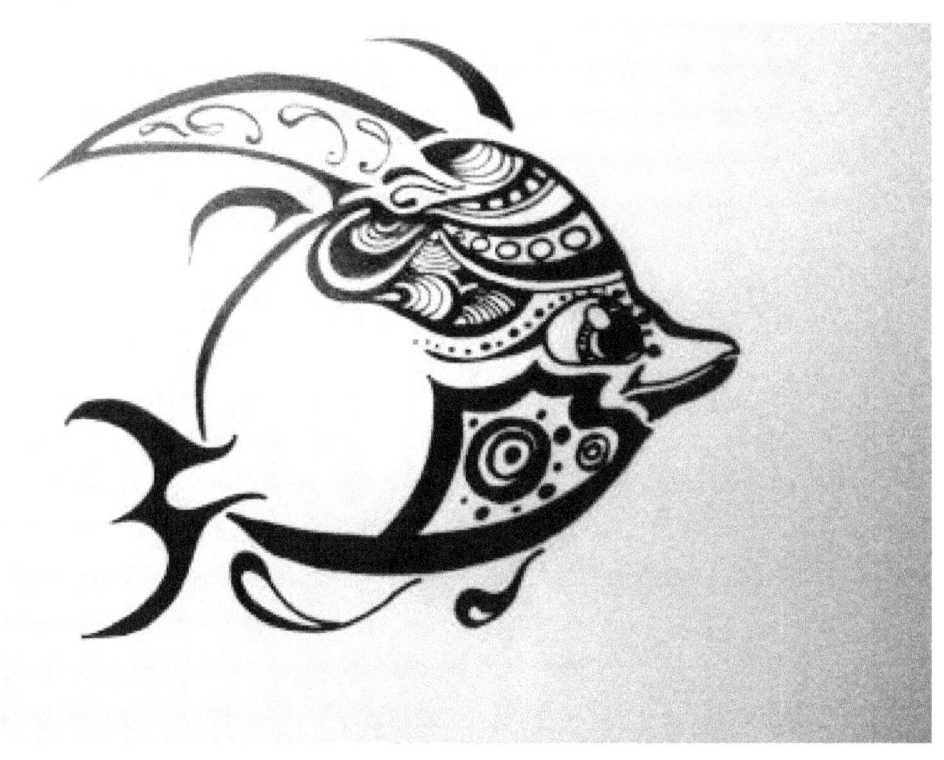

Step 5: Here it is, an amazingly simple and adorable drawing that ought to have turn out resembling this for every one of you. Trust you had a ton of fun drawing a fish folks. Return and go along with me again genuine soon!

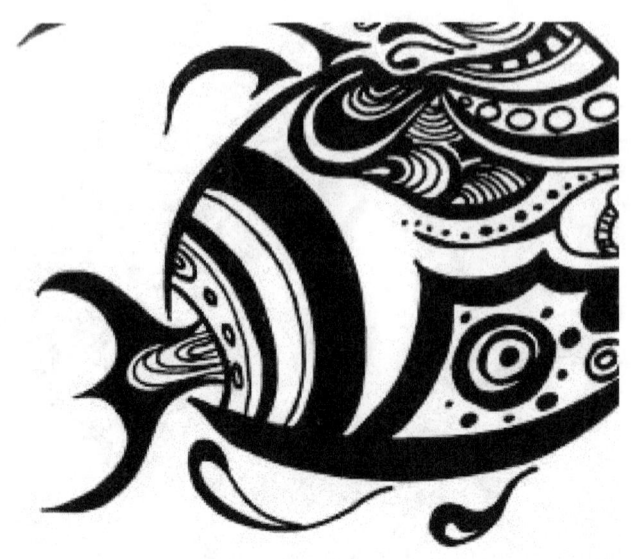

Step 6: You will now start sketching out the state of the fish's face, and body all fit as a fiddle. Notice the score is in the back end for the tail.

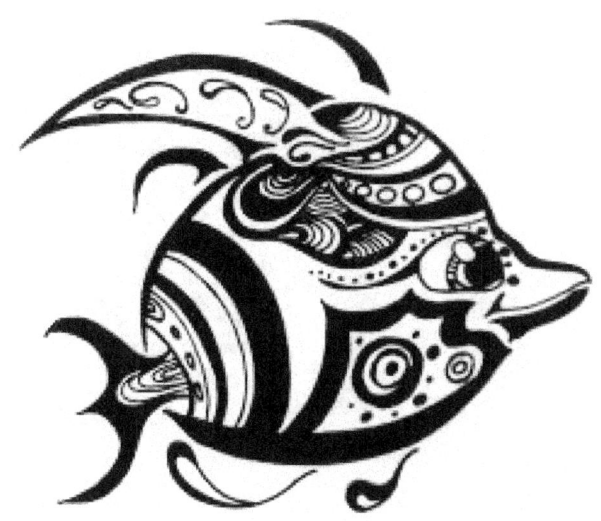

Step 7: Draw the eyes, mouth, and all the balance traces. This is an extremely basic step in light of the fact that all you are doing is making the laid out shapes for everything.

Step 8: Now for your last step, you will include everything else. This incorporates drawing out the eyes, and foreheads, detailing the mouth with a little whirl line, and including every one of the fins striped definition lines to add surface to this creatures hereditary make-up.

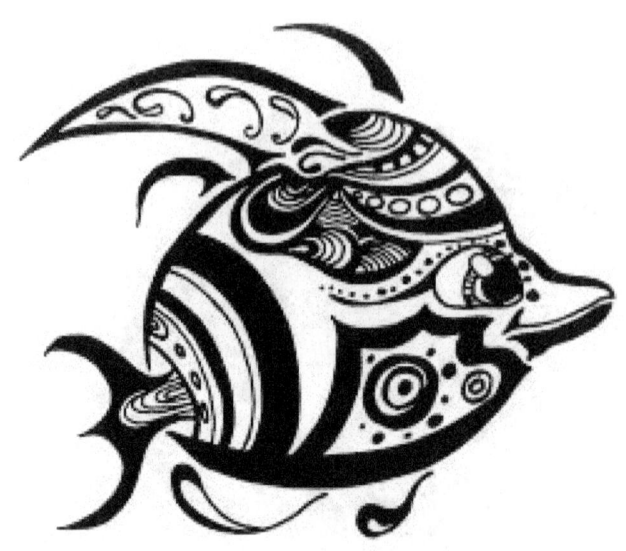

Step 9: Draw the face cover coating which incorporates the flipper, and after that draw the sketched out state of the dorsal blade.

Step 10: Draw out and fill in the fish eye, and after that add some detailing to the fins like you see here. Delete every one of the shapes and lines you attracted step one.

Conclusion

Doodles are an oblivious articulation of our psyche through the craft of jotting and putting pen to paper. We are normally doing or thinking about something else when we doodle. On the telephone, wandering off in fantasy land in school, we are not focusing on what we are drawing. As an outcome doodles are free of any cognizant thought.

Doodles are a phenomenal approach to unleash your imagination. Nowadays as kids we are not urged to draw or to be imaginative unless we are "great at it". Just those that are clearly gifted are urged to draw. You will frequently see people draw geometric shapes when they doodle. They feel good drawing these shapes however they won't generally release themselves and attempt different shapes and styles. Still stress that somebody may see their doodle and it won't be "great".

Doodles don't need to look like anything. There is nobody remaining behind you saying that it is sufficiently bad. When you understand this you can unwind and simply give you a chance to brain meander as your pen makes. You can change any piece of the doodle whenever just by going over what you have officially done. The sky is the point of confinement.

Doodles are an incredible approach to let your psyche unwind and to let your imagination (which is within each one of us) assume control. In the event that you have an issue that needs explaining, let your brain harp on the issue while you let your hand jot on a bit of clear paper. You may be astonished to find that the solution for your issue gets to be evident while you are doodling.

Not just will you're drawing abilities enhance when you doodle yet you won't trust the anxiety alleviation that doodling can give you. It is just barely being recognized that doodling is an extraordinary approach to unwind. In the event that you begin to truly doodle then you will truly see how quiet and push free you feel when you have completed a doodle. As your doodles turn out to be more expound you're sentiment fulfillment will develop and your doodles will form into masterpieces.

Drawing portraits can be precarious particularly in case you're new to drawing. Portraits are trying to draw as a result of the a wide range of parts that need to meet up to depict a visual likeness. For instance, the eyes, ears, lips, nose and face must be corresponding to each other for a representation to have a similarity of the subject.

More apt portraitists know how to catch the embodiment of the face. That implies having the capacity to catch the fine points of interest that depict the character of the face. So it's not as simple as simply drawing some "Hollywood" confronts that look plastic.

In case you're simply beginning, I recommend doing some homework first. Begin by detaching every component and practice until you're fulfilled before moving on. Draw confronts that you're as of now acquainted with. You'll see that well known appearances are less demanding to draw.

Because of the state of your fingers, I suggest that you maintain a strategic distance from long and tiring drawing sessions. You might need to pick something that is brisk to complete, or you might need to arrange you're drawing sessions with the goal that you can finish a solitary drawing in a few shorter sessions. Additionally, you might need to inspire somebody to give you a hand rub previously, then after the fact every drawing session.

In case you're simply beginning, begin with something that is less confounded. Pick dream workmanship that you truly like drawing and continue rehearsing. You can pick one subject, and do whatever it takes not to allude to it as you draw. This will enhance your memory. On the off chance that you overlook the points of interest, you can simply think of your own, since it's dream :)

www.ingramcontent.com/pod-product-compliance
Lightning Source LLC
Chambersburg PA
CBHW080717190526
45169CB00006B/2416